Anonymous

The Arkansas Traveller's Songster

Containing the Celebrated Story of the Arkansas Traveller

Anonymous

The Arkansas Traveller's Songster
Containing the Celebrated Story of the Arkansas Traveller

ISBN/EAN: 9783744794848

Printed in Europe, USA, Canada, Australia, Japan

Cover: Foto ©Thomas Meinert / pixelio.de

More available books at **www.hansebooks.com**

THE

ARKANSAS TRAVELLER'S

SONGSTER:

CONTAINING THE

Celebrated Story of the
Arkansas Traveller,
With the Music for
Violin or Piano,

AND ALSO

An Extensive and
Choice Collection of
New and Popular
Comic and Sentimental Songs.

NEW YORK:

DICK & FITZGERALD, PUBLISHERS,

18 ANN STREET.

Contents.

———o———

ARKANSAS TRAVELLER'S
SONG-BOOK.

---◆◆◆---

THE ARKANSAS TRAVELLER.

By Mose Case.

(Published, in sheet-music form, by BLODGETT & BRADFORD, Music-Publishers, Buffalo.)

THIS piece is intended to represent an Eastern man's experience among the inhabitants of Arkansas, showing their hospitality and the mode of obtaining it.

Several years since, he was travelling the state to Little Rock, the capital. In those days, railroads had not been heard of, and the stage-lines were very limited; so, under the circumstances, he was obliged to travel the whole distance on foot. One evening, about dusk, he came across a small log house, standing fifteen or twenty yards from the road, and enclosed by a low rail fence of the most primitive description. In the doorway sat a man, playing a violin: the tune was the then most popular air in that region—namely, "The Arkansas Traveller." He kept repeating the first part of the tune over and over again, as he could not play the second part. At the time the traveller reached the house it was raining very hard, and he was anxious to obtain shelter from the storm. The house looked like any thing but a shelter, as it was covered with clapboards, and the rain was leaking into every part of it. The old man's daughter Sarah appeared to be getting supper, while a

1*

small boy was setting the table, and the old lady sat in the doorway near her husband, admiring the music.

The stranger, on coming up, said, "How do you do?" The man merely glanced at him, and, continuing to play, replied, "I do as I please."

Stranger. How long have you been living here?

Old Man. D'ye see that mountain thar? Well, that was thar when I come here.

S. Can I stay here to-night?

O. M. No! ye can't stay here.

S. How long will it take me to get to the next tavern?

O. M. Well, you'll not get thar at all, if you stand thar foolin' with me all night! (*Plays.*)

S. Well, how far do you call it to the next tavern?

O. M. I reckon it's upwards of some distance! (*Plays again, as above.*)

S. I am very dry—do you keep any spirits in your house?

O. M. Do you think my house is haunted? They say thar's plenty down in the graveyard. (*Plays as before.*)

S. How do they cross this river ahead?

O. M. The ducks all swim across. (*Plays as before.*)

S. How far is it to the forks of the road?

O. M. I've been livin' here nigh on twenty years, and no road ain't forked yit. (*Plays as before.*)

S. Give me some satisfaction, if you please, sir. Where does this road go to?

O. M. Well, it hain't moved a step since I've been here. (*Plays as before.*)

S. Why don't you cover your house? It leaks.

O. M. 'Cause it's rainin'.

S. Then why don't you cover it when it's not raining?

O. M. 'Cause it don't leak. (*Plays as before.*)

S. Why don't you play the second part of that tune?

O. M. If you're a better player than I am, you can play it yourself. I'll bring the fiddle out to you—I don't want you in here! (*Stranger plays the second part of the tune.*)

O. M. Git over the fence, and come in and sit down—I didn't know you could play. You can board here, if you want to. Kick that dog off that stool, and set down and play it over—I want to hear it agin. (*Stranger plays the second part again.*)

O. M. Our supper is ready now: won't you have some with us?

S. If you please.

O. M. What will you take, tea or coffee?

S. A cup of tea, if you please.

O. M. Sall, git the grubbin'-hoe, and go dig some sassafras, quick! (*Old man plays the first part.*)

S. (*to the little boy*). Bub, give me a knife and fork, if you please.

Boy. We hain't got no knives and forks, sir,

S. Then give me a spoon.

B. We hain't got no spoons neither.

S. Well, then, how do you do?

B. Tolerable, thank you; how do you do, sir? (*Old man plays the first part again!*)

The stranger, finding such poor accommodations, and thinking his condition could be bettered by leaving, soon departed, and at last succeeded in finding a tavern, with better fare. He has never had the courage to visit Arkansas since!

THE DUTCH MUSICIAN.

A Favorite Serio-Comic German Buffo Song.

As sung by TONY PASTOR.

(NOTE.—For the benefit of the English reader, this song is given with the words spelled as pronounced in our language. As it is in the original, a duett, we give it here as such, although sung by Mr. PASTOR as a solo, and with immense success.)

HE.

SHANUS maidschen, wans canst du mauken?
Canst du shpiela? canst du shpiela?

SHE.

Ich can spiel so kliena trummel,
Rub-a-dub-a-dub! dans iest mien trummel!

THE DUTCH MUSICIAN.

HE.

Shanus maidschen, wans canst du mauken?
Canst du shpiela? canst du shpiela?

SHE.

Ich can spiel so kliena fifel,
    Swill-li-willi-wil! dans iest mien fifel!
    Rub-a-dub-a-dub! dans iest mien trummel;
        My swil-li-willi-wil!
        My rub-a-dub-a-dub!
          Dans iest mien trummel!

HE.

Shanus maidschen, wans canst du mauken?
Canst du shpiela? canst du shpiela?

SHE.

Ich can spiel so kliena gyka,
Falla-la-la! dans iest mien gyka;
Swil-li-willi-wil! dans iest mien fifel;
Rub-a-dub-a-dub! dans iest mien trummel;
    My falla-la-la!
    My swil-li-willi-wil!
    My rub-a-dub-a-dub!
        Dans iest mien trummel!

HE.

Shanus maidschen, wans canst du mauken?
Canst du shpiela? canst du shpiela?

SHE.

Ich can spiel so kliena bassgyke—
Zoom-zoom-zoom! dans iest mien bassgyke!
Falla-la-la! dans iest mien gyka;
Swil-li-wil-li-wil! dans iest mien fifel;
Rub-a-dub-a-dub! dans iest mien trummel;
    My zoom-zoom-zoom!
    My falla-la-la!
    My swil-li-willi-wil!
    My rub-a-dub-a-dub!
        Daus iest mien trummel!

HE.

Shanus maidschen, wans canst du mauken?
Canst du shpiela? canst du shpiela?

SHE.

Ich can spiel so kliena bombass—
    Tra-ra-ra! dans iest mien bombass;
    Zoom-zoom-zoom! dans iest mien bassgyke;
    Falla-la-la! dans iest mien gyka!
    Swil-li-willi-wil! dans iest mien fifel;
    Rub-a-dub-a-dub! dans iest mien trummel.
      My tra-ra-ra!
      My zoom-zoom-zoom!
      My falla-la-la!
      My swil-li-willi-wil!
      My rub-a-dub-a-dub!
        Dans iest mien trummel!

HE.

Shanus maidschen, wans canst du mauken?
Canst du shpiela? canst du shpiela?

SHE.

Ich can spiel so kliena triangle—
    Hic-moc-moc! dans iest mien triangle;
    Tra-ra-ra! dans iest mien bombass;
    Zoom-zoom-zoom! dans iest mien bassgyke;
    Falla-la-la! dans iest mien gyka;
    Swil-li-willi-wil! dans iest mien fifel;
    Rub-a-dub-a-dub! dans iest mien trummel;
      My hic-moc-moc!
      My tra-ra-ra!
      My zoom-zoom-zoom!
      My falla-la-la!
      My swil-li-willi-wil!
      My rub-a-dub-a-dub!
        Dans iest mien trummel!

HE.

Shanus maidschen, wans canst du mauken?
Canst du shpiela? canst du shpiela?

SHE.

Ich can spiel so kliena drudlesock—
Qua-qua-qua ! dans iest mien drudlesock ;
Hic-moc-moc ! dans iest mien triangle ;
Tra-ra-ra ! dans iest mien bombass ;
Zoom-zoom-zoom ! dans iest mien bassgyke ;
Falla-la-la ! dans iest mien gyka ;
Swil-li-willi-wil ! dans iest mien fifel ;
Rub-a-dub-a-dub ! daus iest mien trummel.
My qua-qua-qua !
My hic-moc-moc !
My tra-ra-ra !
My zoom-zoom-zoom !
My falla-la-la !
My swil-li-willi-wil !
My rub-a-dub-a-dub !
Dans iest mien trummel !

THE NEUTRAL ENGLISH GENTLEMAN.

AIR—"Fine Old English Gentleman."

ENCRUSTED in his island-home that lies beyond the sea,
Behold the great original and genuine " 'Tis He;"
A paunchy, fuming son of beef, with double weight of chin,
And eyes that were benevolent, but for their singular ten-
    dency to turn green whenever it is remarked that his
    irrepressible American cousins have made another
    treaty with China ahead of him, and taken Albion in—
This neutral English gentleman, one of the modern time.

With William, Duke of Normandy, his ancestors, he boasts,
Came over from the shores of France to whip the Saxon
    hosts:
And this he makes a source of pride; but wherefore there
    should be
Such credit to an Englishman, in the fact that he is de-
    scended from a nation which England is forever pre-
    tending to regard as slightly her inferior in every

thing, and particularly behind her in military and naval affairs, we cannot really see—
This neutral English gentleman, one of the modern time.

He deals in Christianity—Episcopalian brand—
And sends his missionaries forth to bully heathen-land;
Just mention "slavery" to him, and, with a joyous sigh,
He'll say it's 'orrid, scandalous, although he is ready to
    fight for the cotton raised by slaves, and forgets how
    he bothered the Chinese to make them take opium;
    and blew the Sepoys from the guns because the poor
    devils refused to be enslaved by the East India Com-
    pany, or phi-lan-thro-py—
This neutral English gentleman, one of the modern time.

He yields to Brother Jonathan a love that passeth show:
" We're Hanglo-Saxons, both of us, and can't be foes, you
    know"—
But, as a Christian gentleman, he cannot, cannot hide
His horror of the spectacle of four millions of black beings
    being held in bondage by a nation professing the largest
    liberty in the world; though, in case of an anti-slavery
    crusade, the interest of his Manchester factors would
    imperatively forbid him to take part on either side—
This neutral English gentleman, one of the modern time.

Now seeing the said Jonathan by base rebellion stirred,
And battling with pro-slavery, it might be thence inferred
That British hearts would be with us in this most holy strife;
But instead of that, John Bull's sympathy is labelled " Neu-
    trality," and consigned to any rebel port not too closely
    blockaded to permit English vessels loaded with muni-
    tions to slip in. And when you ask Mr. Bull what he
    meant by his inconsistent conduct, he becomes notori-
    ously indignant, rolls up his eyes, and says, "I can't
    endure to see brothers murdering each other, and keep-
    ing me out of my cotton—I can't, upon my life"—
This neutral British gentleman, one of the modern time.

Supposing Mr. Bull should die, the question might arise,
" Will he be wanted down below, or wafted to the skies?"
  2

Allowing that he had his choice, it really seems to me,
The moral English gentleman would choose a front seat
  with his Iufernal Majesty: since Milton, in his blank-
  verse correspondence with old Time, more than once
  hinted the possibility of Nick's rebellion against Heaven
  succeediug. And as the Lower Secessia has cottoned
  to England through numerous Hanoverian reigns, such
  a choice on the part of the philanthropical Britisher
  would be simply another specimen of his neutral-i-ty—
The neutral British gentleman, one of the modern time.

THE SEVEN DAYS' FIGHT.

Aɪʀ—"Louisiana Lowlands."

'Wᴀʏ down in Old Virginia, not many months ago,
McClellan made a movement—he made it very slow;
The rebels they soon found it out, and pitched into our rear;
They got the very d—l, for they found old Kearney there !

Chorus.

In the old Virginia Lowlands, Lowlands, Lowlands,
In the old Virginia Lowlands, low !

Again at Savage' Station, we met the rebel foe—
That General Sumner whipped them, their list of killed will
    show ;
Then "Fighting Josy Hooker" came up with his train—
He met them on the third day, and whipped them over
    again.
            In the old, etc.

The rebels they still followed us, their numbers two to one,
But Little Mac he let them know that Yankees would not
    run.
Mac thought that he would stop the fun, and bring it to an
    end—
The only way to do that was, for Couch's men to send.
            In the old, etc.

When we heard that Mac had sent for us, with joy our
    hearts did fill,
And we were quickly ready on the top of Malvern hill;
The rebels they commenced the fight, but we were not dis-
    mayed—
They might as well have met the de'il, as Howe and his
    brigade!
        In the old, etc.

The rebels they began the fight by throwing shot and
    shell:
That was a game, they soon found out, that Couch's men
    could them excel.
We fought them from the morning's dawn until the setting
    sun—
Among the killed and wounded, why, they had three to
    one!
        In the old, etc.

The Ninety-third—the Twenty-third—were early on the
    ground;
The Sixty-first, New York Chasseurs, soon showed them-
    selves around;
Then came the First Long Island—we all did our work
    quite well,
As many a wounded rebel from experience can tell.
        In the old, etc.

When we came to James River, the boys began to cheer,
As they saw the little Monitor—up the river she did steer.
The rebel General got scared, and unto his men did say—
"Here comes a Yankee earthquake, we'd better get away."
        In the old, etc.

Now, all ye politicians, a word I have for you:
Let our Little Mac alone, for he is tried and true;
And you have found out lately that he is our only hope—
For twice he saved the capital—likewise McDowell and
    Pope.
        In the old, etc.

Now I think I will finish, and bring it to an end,
With three cheers for Little Mac—he's every soldier's
    friend:
I would like all agitators and politicians to understand,
If one can save the Union, why Little Mac's the man.
            In the old, etc.

———

MONEY IS YOUR ONLY FRIEND.

A Matter-of-Fact Comic Song.

Air—" Green grow the Rushes, O !"

. Of friendship I have heard much talk;
    But you will find it, in the end,
That if distressed at any time,
    Then money is your only friend.
Chorus—Yes, money is your only friend,
        Money is your only friend;
        Where'er you go, you'll find it so—
          You must have money for to spend.

If you are sick, and like to die,
    And for the doctor then you send,
You must to him advance a fee—
    Then money is your only friend.
              Yes, money, etc.

If you should have a suit at law,
    On which you all your hopes depend,
The lawyers want to see your cash—
    Then money is your only friend.
              Yes, money, etc.

Then let me have a store of gold,
    From every ill it will defend:
In every exigence of life,
    Dear money is your only friend.
              Yes, money, etc.

THE THEATRE ON A BENEFIT NIGHT;

Or, the Bowery Third Tier.

AIR—"Paddy's Curiosity-Shop."

MR. BLUBBS is my name, you must know,
    And I'm a genteel sort of man;
A nice little wife I have got,
    Whom I always treat when I can.
To the theatre we went 'tother night—
    'Twas a benefit night, d'ye see;
A rich treat I thought we should have,
    And so thought my sweet Mrs. B.

Chorus.

There's a small chance of seeing the sights,
    It's a fact, as my song it will show,
To those who on benefit nights
    To the Bowery Theatre will go.

'Twas six when our lodgings we left,
    And to the theatre we went;
But the crowd there it soon got so great,
    All manner of shapes we were bent.
At length up the stairs we were crammed —
    Some joked, and called it a spree,
To see how my limbs they were jammed,
    In protecting my dear Mrs. B.
            There's a small chance, etc.

In the third tier we quickly were poked;
    Of our purses we both soon were eased;
We were stuck 'mongst a lot of fast ladies,
    Who seemed to act just as they pleased.
The place was so dreadfully hot,
    With myself, 'gad, it didn't agree;
It soon made me awfully sick,
    And so it made poor Mrs. B.
            There's a small chance, etc.

2*

We didn't know what for to do,
    For we couldn't make our way out;
We were jammed up like plums in a pudding,
    And were shamefully knocked all about.
" You fool, take your hat off !" says one;
    And another, alluding to me,
Says, " I wonder where he picked *her* up?"
    What an insult to poor Mrs. B. !
          There's a small chance, etc.

At last we got settled a bit,
    Not heeding at all what was said;
But we hadn't been sitting down long,
    When I got such a thump on the head !
My hat was knocked over my eyes,
    And I was quickly unable to see:
" Lord ! I want to skedaddle," says I ;
    " So do I," says my dear Mrs. B.
          There's a small chance, etc.

We managed to squeeze our way out—
    My nose being nearly cut in two;
My wife's clothes were all sadly torn,
    And my visage was quite black and blue.
I went off to get my wounds dressed,
    But the doctor first asked for his fee :
I hadn't a postage-stamp left,
    And neither had poor Mrs. B.
          There's a small chance, etc.

We made the best haste to our home,
    And a pretty nice state we were in—
Broken nose, broken bonnet and hat,
    And our pockets both eased of their tin !
And, although we went to the play,
    Not the first single scene did we see:
I ne'er went to the theatre since,
    Nor I never brought sweet Mrs. B.
          There's a small chance, etc.

ALL MANKIND ARE WORMS.

A highly Popular Comic Song.

Sung by all the Comic Vocalists.

Air—" Bow, wow, wow !"

As all we mortals turn to clay,
　When closed our mortal terms, sir,
I think we may with reason say
　That all mankind are worms, sir.
But as there's some may doubt this truth,
　And I like to be exact, sir,
Your patience kindly grant me, while
　I'll try to prove the fact, sir.
　　　　Chorus—Bow, wow, wow, etc.

The Dandy he's a tape-worm,
　Made up of stays and lace, sir;
The Tailor he's a cabbage-worm,
　That cuts your leaves with grace, sir.
The Lover he's a glow-worm,
　That shines but to allure, sir;
The Husband he's a ring-worm,
　That old wives best can cure, sir.
　　　　Bow, wow, wow, etc.

The Glutton he's a meal-worm,
　Still feeding night and day, sir;
The Drunkard he's a still-worm,
　That drinks his all away, sir.
The Brewer he's a malt-worm,
　A very jolly one, sir;
The Farmer he's a grub-worm,
　That grubs on in the sun, sir.
　　　　Bow, wow, wow, etc.

The Scholar he's a book-worm,
　That best on learning feeds, sir;
The Miser he's a muck-worm,
　That on a dunghill breeds, sir.

The Rogue he's but a blind-worm,
   That works on in the dark, sir;
The Coquette she's a bait-worm,
   That angles for a spark, sir.
           Bow, wow, wow, etc.

The Idler he's a slow-worm,
   With laziness he's rife, sir;
The Soldier he's a blood-worm,
   Still feeding upon life, sir!
A Maid she is a silk-worm,
   That changes every way, sir;
And Love "a worm i' the bud" is,
   That eats our peace away, sir.
           Bow, wow, wow, etc.

And thus I think I've proved to you
   That all mankind are worms, sir—
Of different kinds and natures, too,
   And different shapes and forms, sir:
And since that all our bodies go
   To the worms at our tail-end, sir,
Let's hope, like jolly butterflies,
   That we may all ascend, sir!
           Bow, wow, wow, etc.

THE WEDDED BACHELOR.

A New Parody.

NOT a drum was heard, not a signal-note,
   As the parties to the altar we hurried;
But each person took their farewell look
   Of the bachelor about to be married.

We married him quickly, at dead of night,
   The state of bachelorhood turning,
By the struggling moonbeams' misty light,
   And our candles dimly burning.

No useless satins enclosed his breast,
   Nor did costly attire surround him;
But, true to the bachelor's plain style of dress,
   And the priest's cloak folded around him.

Few and short were the prayers we said,
   And we spoke not a word of sorrow;
But, as we gazed in his face, we plainly read
   That he bitterly thought of the morrow!

We thought, as we stroked down his narrow bed,
   And smoothed his lonely pillow,
How the mop and the broomstick would fly o'er his head,
   And we far away on the billow.

Lightly they'll talk of the one that's gone,
   And before his dear spouse upbraid him;
But they'll little expect, if they let him pass on,
   He'll follow the samples they've made him.

But half of our heavy task was done,
   · When the bell tolled the hour for retiring;
And we knew, by the jingling and rattling of tins,
   That a horning was about transpiring.

Sadly and dearly he did repent
   Of the step taken in matrimony;
Almost broken-hearted he did lament—
   " Oh, leave me ALONE for my glory!"

PADDY O'FLANAGAN.

'TWAS Paddy O'Flanagan set out one morning
   From Dublin, sweet city, to London on foot,
In an old tattered jacket, all foppery scorning,
   With a shoe on his leg and his neck in a boot.
Musha whack! in no time he walked over the water,
   And soon set his head on England's famed shore;
While for joy of his safety his stomach did totter—
   He sung Teddy O'Reilly and Molly Asthore,

With his phililu hubbuboo hugamaurainee,
  Musha gra, botheration, and smalliloo huh!

A place he soon got when in London arrived, sir,
  To brush up a gemman, and wait on his coat—
Where he soon learned to know that jist four beans make
    five, sir,
  And could tell you a tale with his tongue down his throat.
Now one day, while Pat was his master attending,
  In his study, where letters around him did lay,
When he begged hard for one to his friends to be sending,
  As 'twould save him from writing, and be the best way.
              With his phililu, etc.

Soon after, being sent with a basket and letter,
  Crammed full of live pigeons to give to a friend,
Enraged at their fluttering, he thought it was better
  To set them at large, and their misery end:
Then on, jog he went, to the place where directed,
  But the door had no knocker—so, what does he do?
'Faith, he knocked at the next, where the servant attend-
      ing—
Cried Pat, "It's your knocker I want, and not you!"
              With your phililu, etc.

Being brought 'fore the gemman, he gave him the note,
  Who said, "In the letter here's pigeons, I find."
"Be jabers," says Pat, "that's a very good joke,
  For they fled from the basket, and left me behind!"
The gentleman swore for the loss he must pay,
  Or on losing his place for certain depend;
Pat replied, "To your offer I'll not once say nay,
  If you'll be so kind as the money to lend!"
              With my phililu, etc.

Being pleased with the joke, poor Pat got forgiven,
  For, though blunder on blunder, no harm there was
      meant:
And if he's not dead, with his master he's living—
  And when not out of humor, is always content.

Nay, more, Paddy Flanagan joins in the wish
That the cares of our friends may soon find a decrease;
That war may be drowned on dry land with the fish,
And the world forever taste blessings of peace.

    With my phililu, etc.

KATTY O'RANN.

Was not Patrick O'Lilt, sure, a broth of a lad,
Who bartered what money and baubles he had,
 For the love of his sweetheart, Miss Katty O'Rann?
Since he fell deep in love, 'faith! no longer the spade
He handled, or followed the turf-cutting trade;
But sang day and night to make his heart light,
And swore for his Katty he'd die or he'd fight:
 Thus did Patrick O'Lilt for Miss Katty O'Rann.

    Chorus—Ri tol de rol, etc.

He sang out his love in a sorrowful strain;
His warbling she heard, but she laughed at his pain—
 Which he could not bear from Miss Katty O'Rann.
'Twas enough to have melted the heart of a stone
To have heard the poor lad sing, sigh, mutter, and moan,
While she turned up her nose, which stood always awry,
And plump on another she cast her sheep's eye,
 Crying, "Pat, you won't do for Miss Katty O'Rann."

    Ri tol de rol, etc.

As he found no impression he made on the maid,
'Faith, he shovelled himself out of life with his spade,
 Determined to perish for Katty O'Rann:
For, with spade, axe, and mallet, about his neck tied,
He plunged in the Liffey, and there for her died!
As he sunk from the shore, he cried, "Katty, no more
Shall you trouble my spirit, or make my bones sore;
 So bad luck to you, beautiful Katty O'Rann!"

    Ri tol de rol, etc.

PHILIP THE FALCONER.

Young Philip the falconer's up with the day,
  With his merlin on his arm,
And down the mill meadows has taken his way
  To hawk—and pray where's the harm?
Philip is stalwart, and Philip is young,
And Philip, they say, has a musical tongue.
The miller's young sister is fresh and is fair,
And Philip he always is hawking there!
For he vows and declares, believe it or not,
There's not in the kingdom, for herons, such a spot;
And falcons, they say, to fly true to their prey,
Should be trained in the morning early.

The miller's to market to buy him some corn,
  For work it should never stand still;
A maiden is loitering under the thorn,
  In the meadow below the mill;
And Philip's grown tired of a bachelor's life—
Thinks the miller's young sister would make a good wife:
And so comes a whisper, and so comes a smile,
And then a long leave-taking over the stile.
Oh, when he returns from market, I guess,
The miller will find he's a sister the less!
For maidens, they say, do not always say "Nay,"
When they're asked in the morning early.

The miller's returned to a comfortless home,
  No maiden's sweet voice is there;
He sought o'er the hills, through the valleys and fields,
  For comfort his spirits to cheer.
But the birds sang less sweetly, the streams murmured low,
The winds were all cross, and the mill wouldn't go:
But he met little Mary just down by the lea— [hearts free;
Now they both had long loved, when they thought their
"O Mary," he said, and her hand pressed the while,
"Shall we talk of our wedding just down by the stile?"
She blushed, turned away, but she didn't say "Nay,"
So they married one morning early.

SHE WAS SISTER TO THE ANGELS.

SHE was sister to the angels—
  For we knew we could not trace,
In that form of radiant beauty,
  Any stain of earthly race;
Like a sunbeam was her laughter,
  And of heaven's own blue her eye;
And we wondered not they took her
  To their home beyond the sky:
Like a shadow that comes flitting
  Through some bright and sunny beam,
She has passed away before us,
  And has left us but a dream.

There are flowers that fade in summer,
  That the spring-time may restore;
But the heart grows sad and weary,
  Ere the winter-time is o'er.
In a thousand sunny places
  We their beauteous forms may view;
But they seem not half so lovely
  As the flowers our childhood knew.
So in all that's fair around us,
  We in part recall that face,
That had less of earth than heaven,
  Yet of each had left a trace.

JAKE SCHNEIDER'S DAUGHTER.

A Parody on "Lord Ullin's Daughter."

By JOHN F. POOLE.

Mit der Tune of "Whack row de dow."

A VELLER, in der Jersey clime,
  Cries, "Poatman, do not darry!
Un I'll gif you a pretzel vine
  To row us o'er der verry."

3

"Now who vould cross der Shersey creek,
Dis dark und muddy vater?"
"Oh, I'm Von Schunk," der veller shpeak;
"Un dis Jake Schneider's daughter."

Chorus.

Whack row de dow,
A hunkey boy vos Jacob Schneider;
Whack row de dow,
De gal vos shtole avay!

"Ve've left her vader's house pehind—
Across der shtream I'll dake her;
Un if der minishder ve vind,
Mrs. Von Schunk I'll make her.
Old Schneider's men pehind us ride,
Dey shvear dey'll cut mine vizen!
Den who vill sheer mine ponny pride,
If I am daked to brison?"

Whack row de dow, etc.

Out shpoke der poatman, "You sha'nt vail;
To go, by tam, I'm ready!
It ish not vor your pretzel shtale,
But vor your bretty lady.
Shust help der poat vrom off dese logs—
Too heavy 'tis to carry;
Un, dough der mud ish vull of vrogs,
I'll row you o'er der verry."

Whack row de dow, etc.

Shust den der rain pegin'd to vall—
Der pullvrogs shtopped deir squeaking;
Der lady virst mit vright did bawl,
Der vet soon set her shrieking.
Un den, ash louder plowed der vind,
Un ash der night grow'd drearer,
Dey heard der Deutschenmen pehind—
Deir drampling sounded nearer!

Whack row de dow, etc.

"Hurry up your gakes!" der lady said,
  " Dough dempests round us gader;
I doesn't vant,a proken head,⦁
  Un so von't meet mine vader."
Der poat vos launched ubon der creek,
  Der lovers vent on poard it;
Der vaters rushed in trough each leak,
  Un loud der shtorm roared it.
          Whack row de dow, etc.

Un ven half vay across dey got,
  Trough mud un vater shteering,
Olt Schneider reached der vatal shpot,
  His wrath vos changed to shvearing.
For in der poat, in her pest clothes,
  His shild he did disbgover;
Von lovely hand shtretched vrom her nose,
  Un von vos rount her lover.
          Whack row de dow, etc.

"Gome pack, gome pack!" alout he cried,
  "Vorgive your volly I vill."
"Nien! nary pack!" Von Schunk replied,
  " You may go to der tuyfel!"
Der lovers vent. He turned around,
  Mit curses loud un blenty,
Vent to his home, and dere he vound
  His money-trawer vos empty.
          Whack row de dow, etc.

MY OWN NATIVE LAND.

I've roved over mountain, I've crossed over flood;
  I've traversed the wave-rolling sand:
Though the fields were as green, and the moon shone as
    bright,
  Yet it was not my own native land.
      No, no, no, no, no—no, no, no, no, no!

Though the fields were as green, and the moon shone as
    bright,
  Yet it was not my own native land.

The right hand of friendship how oft I have grasped,
  And bright eyes have smiled and looked bland;
Yet happier far were the hours that I passed
  In the West—in my own native land.
      Yes, yes, yes, yes, yes—yes, yes, yes, yes, yes!
Yet happier far were the hours that I passed
  In the West—in my own native land.

Then hail, dear Columbia, the land that we love,
  Where flourishes Liberty's tree;
The birthplace of Freedom, our own native home,
  'Tis the land, 'tis the land of the free!
      Yes, yes, yes, yes, yes—yes, yes, yes, yes, yes!
The birthplace of Freedom, our own native home,
  'Tis the land, 'tis the land of the free!

THE SHIELD, THE FISHBALL, AND THE SEWING-MACHINE;

Or, Love, Arsenic, and Percussion-Caps.

Written and sung, with unusual applause, by TONY PASTOR, the famous clown and comic vocalist.

AIR—"In the Merry Month of May."

MY song is of a "Peeler" gay,
  A fancy chap that once I knew,
His "beat" 'twas up and down Broadway,
  And he looked so fine in his suit of blue!
The girls would smile as he'd pass by;
But one there was that met his eye—
He thought her the fairest that ever he'd seen—
She worked in a shop on a sewing-machine.
    (*Spoken.*) Big thing on the sewing-machine.
      Chorus—My song, etc.

Each even she'd come at six o'clock,
  The Peeler for her would wait the while;
The wagons and stages at once he'd stop,
  And hand her across with a wink and a smile.
But he had a rival, five feet in his boots,
A sort of a cook down at Meschutt's;
A nice young man of limited means—
He was chief-engineer of the pork and beans!
          Big thing on the pork and beans.
                  My song, etc.

Says the Peeler, "I'll cut out this 'Fishball.'"
  To "Sewing-Machine" he showed the cash;
Upon her each night he used to call,
  Which quickly settled poor Cooky's hash.
One night he called, the maid to see,
And found her squat on the Peeler's knee;
And, what with affright there made him stand,
She was playing away with his club in her hand.
          Big thing on the club.
                  My song, etc.

Cried he, "For to live is now no use!"—
  He crept into the coffee-can through the spout;
But, without ever cooking poor Cooky's goose,
  He was only half boiled when the fire went out.
But, as he was resolved to die,
He swallowed the shell of an oyster-pie,
Then rammed it down with a loaf of bread—
It stuck in his throat, and choked him dead!
          Big thing on the Cooky.
                  My song, etc.

When "Sewing-Machine" the news did hear,
  For a pound of arsenic she went out;
She drank it off in a quart of beer,
  And threw up till she turned right inside out!
When the Peeler heard of these sad mishaps,
He swallowed a pound of percussion-caps;
  3*

Then a gallon of brandy his heat increases,
Till they bursted and blew him all to pieces!
     Big thing on the percussions.
       My song, etc.

LITTLE MORE CIDER.

I LOVE the white girl and the black,
 And I love all the rest;
I love the girls for loving me,
 But I love myself the best.
Oh, dear, I am so thirsty!
 I've just been down to supper—
I drank three pails of apple-jack,
 And a tub of apple-butter!

Chorus—Oh, little more cider too,
  A little more cider too;
  A little more cider for Miss Dinah,
  A little more cider too!

When first I saw Miss Snowflake,
 'Twas on Broadway I spied her;
I'd give my hat and boots, I would,
 If I could been beside her.
She looked at me, and I looked at her,
 And then I crossed the street;
And then she smiling said to me,
 "A little more cider sweet."
    Oh, little more cider, etc.

Oh, I wish I was an apple,
 And Snowflake was another;
Oh, what a pretty pair we'd make,
 Upon a tree together!
How bad de darkeys all would feel,
 When on the tree they spied her,
To think how happy we would be
 When we're made into cider!
    Oh, little more cider, etc.

But now old age comes creeping on—
  We grow down, and don't get bigger;
And cider sweet am sour then,
  And I am just de nigger.
But let de cause be what it will,
  Short, small, or wider,
She am de apple of my soul,
  And I'm bound to be beside her.
          Oh, little more cider, etc.

KATHLEEN O'REGAN.

A boy in my teens, just before I reached twenty,
  Among the young lasses would cast a hawk's eye:
Fresh lilies and roses, and posies in plenty,
  Graced Kathleen O'Regan, the pride of Athy.
She'd say, "Pat, be aisy! ah, why do you teaze me?
  I dread to come near you, and cannot tell why."
"My sowl! neither Jenny nor Nell of Kilkenny
  Are dear as sweet Kathleen, the pride of Athy."

"Arrah, Pat, you know that my father and mother
  Both think me too young to be married—oh, fie!
To stay awhile longer I know they would rather;
  Then can't you have patience?"—"Dear Kathleen, not I."
She smiled like a Cupid, which made me look stupid—
  My eyes fixed with love, when I found she'd comply;
So bloomed every feature, like soft tints of Nature,
  Of Kathleen O'Regan, the pride of Athy.

Then war drove me on to where battle was raging,
  She kissed me, I pressed her with tears in each eye:
We sighed, groaned, and blubbered—she cried so engaging,
  "Remember poor Kathleen, and once-loved Athy,
Where oft, in its bowers, you've pulled me sweet flowers—
  If e'er you forget it, I'll certainly die!"
"My Kathleen, to you, love, I'll ever be true, love,
  Sweet Kathleen O'Regan, the pride of Athy."

A LITTLE SONG OF LITTLE THINGS.

A Little Comic Ditty,

Sung by the late JOHN WINANS, at the National and Bowery Theatres.

AIR—"Fine Old Irish Gentleman."

I'LL sing to you a little song, in little jingling rhymes,
'Bout little folks and little things in these funny little times,
Their little ways, their little deeds—though perhaps I've
    little cause,
And very little skill, indeed, to merit your applause—
    For this is a little history of little modern times.

The little joys of former times have nearly passed away;
There's very little labor now, and very little pay:
All things with being little here we honestly may charge,
If we except the taxes, which you'll own are very large—
              For this is, etc.

We've very little orators, who take no little pains
To show the world at large that they have very little brains;
We've little men in Congress, who are no little bore,
Besides a little bank-bill to oppress the little poor—
              For this is, etc.

We've little swells about the town, who've a very little
    purse;
And pert and prudish little maids, with a little child at
    nurse;
And little foppish dandy sparks, whose credit's very queer,
Who strut their little forms about to quiz the little fair—
              For this is, etc.

And then we've pretty little girls, who pore o'er little
    sonnets,
With little waists and little feet, and little fancy bonnets,
Who paint their pretty little cheeks, and play their little
    parts,
To win the little men's sweet smiles, and please their little
    hearts—   For this is, etc.

We've little balls and little routs, where little people go,
To sport their little figures and to sport their little toe;
Little sparks and little clerks, just broke from their mamma;
And little boys who think they're men, with a little sweet
    cigar—
                For this is, etc.

A little smart apology, and then my song is done:
I've spoke a little freely, just to cause a little fun;
My object being, of little devils blue all to disarm,
So if I've gained that little end, I've done but little harm
    In this my little history of little modern times.

TIT FOR TAT.

A highly Popular Comic Song.

Sung by all the celebrated vocalists.

AIR—"The Tickling-Man."

MR. TIBBS, as they tell me, was not half so bold
As his gay little wife, a most terrible scold,
    Who was witty, and pretty, and smart, and all that:
But in truth she'd some reason to scold, I'm afraid,
For she lately detected him kissing the maid!
So he very much stared when she told him one day—
"My love, if you like, you may go to the play,
    Which is witty, and pretty, and smart, and all that."

Now Tibbs was a lover of plays that were witty,
But much more in love with his wife's maid, sweet Kitty,
    Who was witty, and pretty, and smart, and all that.
With lawless emotion his bosom now burned,
And in secret, alone, by the garden returned;
The moon, with her horns, was just rising to view—
Fatal vision, which told him that he was horned too!
    Though so witty, and pretty, and smart, and all that.

Ye gods! at that moment his optics descried
His wife, with a tall, dashing youth at her side,
  Who was witty, and pretty, and smart, and all that.
Mr. Tibbs, bolting out, cried, with dreadful grimace,
"Vile woman! now dare look your spouse in the face!"
She screamed, and exclaimed, "You base wretch! in good
    time
My maid has confessed all your wicked design—
  For she's witty, and pretty, and smart, and all that.

"I'm resolved on revenge—I your steps have waylaid,
And my cousin, the captain, I've brought to my aid—
  He is witty, and pretty, and smart, and all that;
With him you may settle the case in dispute,
And I'll give you, gratis, this lesson to boot:
When next with my maid you would kiss, and all that,
Pray remember your wife may return 'tit for tat,'
  If she's witty, and pretty, and smart, and all that!"

HIGHLAND MARY.

Ye banks, and braes, and streams around
  The castle o' Montgomery,
Green be your woods, and fair your flowers,
  Your waters never drumlie!
There Simmer faust unfauld her robes
  And there the langest tarry;
For there I took the last fareweel
  O' my sweet Highland Mary.

How sweetly bloomed the gay green birk,
  How rich the hawthorn's blossom,
As, underneath their fragrant shade,
  I clasped her to my bosom!
The golden hours, on angel-wings,
  Flew o'er me and my dearie;
For dear to me as light and life
  Was my sweet Highland Mary.

Wi' monie a vow and locked embrace,
    Our parting was fu' tender;
And pledging aft to meet again,
    We tore oursels asunder:
But oh, fell Death's untimely frost,
    That nipped my flower sae early!
Now green's the sod and cauld's the clay
    That wraps my Highland Mary!

Oh, pale, pale now those rosy lips,
    I aft hae kissed sae fondly!
And closed for aye the sparkling glance
    That dwelt on me sae kindly!
And mouldering now in silent dust,
    That heart that lo'ed me dearly;
But still within my bosom's core
    Shall live my Highland Mary.

AM I NOT FONDLY THINE OWN?

THOU, thou, reign'st in this bosom—
    There, there, hast thou thy throne;
Thou, thou, know'st that I love thee—
    Am I not fondly thine own?
Yes, yes, yes, yes, am I not fondly thine own?

Then, then, e'en as I love thee,
    Say, say, wilt thou love me?
Thoughts, thoughts, tender and true, love,
    Say wilt thou cherish for me?
Yes, yes, yes, yes, say wilt thou cherish for me?

Speak, speak, love, I implore thee!
    Say, say, hope shall be thine:
- Thou, thou, know'st that I love thee—
    Say but thou wilt be mine!
Yes, yes, yes, yes, say but thou wilt be mine.

I'D BE A BLUE-BOTTLE.

A Popular Parody.

Sung by Mr. J. REEVE, in Buckstone's Burletta, "Billy Taylor."

AIR—"I'd be a Butterfly."

I'D he a blue-bottle, buzzing and blue,
With a chimy proboscis, and nothing to do
But to dirty white dimity curtains, and blow
The choicest of meats when the summer days glow.
Let the hater of sentiment, dewdrops, and flowers,
Scorn the insect that flutters in sunbeams and bowers;
There's a pleasure which none but the blue-bottle knows—
'Tis to buzz in the ear of a man in a doze!

How charming to haunt a sick-chamber, and revel
O'er the invalid's pillow, like any blue devil!
When pursued, to bounce off to the window, and then
From the pane to the counterpane bounce back again!
   I'd be a blue-bottle, buzzing and blue,
   With a chimy proboscis, and nothing to do
   But to dirty white dimity curtains, and blow
   The choicest of meats when the summer days glow!

COME, SIT THEE DOWN.

COME, sit thee down, my bonny, bonny love,
  Come, sit thee down, by me, love,
And I will tell thee many a tale
  Of the dangers of the sea;
Of the perils of the deep, love,
  Where angry tempests roar,
And the raging billows wildly dash
  Upon the groaning shore!
    Come, sit thee down, my bonny, bonny love,
    Come, sit thee down by me, love,
    And I will tell thee many a tale
    Of the dangers of the sea.

The skies are flaming red, my love,
   The skies are flaming red, love,
And darkly rolls the mountain-wave,
   And rears its monstrous head;
While skies and ocean blending,
   And bitter howls the blast—
And one daring tar, 'twixt life and death,
   Clings to the shattered mast!

            Come, sit thee down, etc.

A VERY GOOD HAND AT IT.

A Favorite Comic Song.

Sung by WILLIAM REEVE, comedian and comic vocalist.

AIR—" Jeremy Diddler."

To New York I just came 'tother day,
   With my pockets all laden with cash, sirs;
I soon took a walk through Broadway,
   For I thought I would cut such a dash, sirs.
There I met with Miss Emily Lee,
   And an " open house" being quite handy,
I asked her to step in with me,
   And there take a small drop of brandy.

            Chorus—Tol lol de rol, etc.

She quickly then gave her consent—
   We went in, and to drink did begin it:
She ordered a bottle of wine,
   And guzzled it off in a minute!
At that I began to look blue—
   Thinks I, " Now it's no use to stand at it."
Says she, " Sir, believe me—it's true—
   I'm reckoned a very good hand at it!"

            Tol lol de rol, etc.

4

Then she said that her stomach felt queer—
  Some victuals would give it relief, sirs;
Then she knocked in just five oyster-stews,
  Then a large plate or two of roast beef, sirs.
She said that the lobsters looked nice—
  If I'd be so kind as to stand a bit;
She bolted óff two in a trice,
  For she's reckoned a very good hand at it.
                    Tol lol de rol, etc.

We wandered the streets all the day,
  And saw what sights there were to see;
At length unto me she did say,
  " I should like a good strong cup of tea."
We quick headed off for Meschutt's—
  To walk in we didn't long stand at it;
There she took tea and cakes for an hour—
  Oh, she's reckoned a very good hand at it!
                    Tol lol de rol, etc.

Then next pork and beans caught her eye,
  So she called up the waiter so swellish,
And ordered a very large plate,
  With an oyster-pie just for a relish!
She then took a fancy to hash,
  And asked me if I wouldn't stand a bit;
She swallowed just six plates of that,
  For she's reckoned a very good hand at it.
                    Tol lol de rol, etc.

I found I was wanting some rest,
  So I thought I'd look out for a bed, sirs;
She said that she thought 'twould be best,
  If I'd occupy half hers instead, sirs.
In a moment I gave my consent—
  Her dwelling it was rather grand a bit;
'Twas tasty and nice, and all that,
  For she's reckoned a very good hand at it.
                    Tol lol de rol, etc.

Next morning quite early I rose,
  But I found such a pain in my head, sirs!
She had bolted away with my clothes,
  And left me alone in the bed, sirs.
So, young men, I beg you take care,
  And love from your knobs pray abandon it;
Or, like me, you'll be caught in a snare,
  By one that's a very good hand at it.
                    Tol lol de rol, etc.

CHISELLING THE BURIAL-CLUB.

Air—"Paddy's Curiosity-Shop."

My old woman one day says to me,
  "A thought has popped into my head—
How hard up our young ones would be,
  If supposing as how you was dead!"
Says I, "Old gal, tip us your fin—
  You shall never be hard up for grub·
For to-morrow I'll muster some tin,
  And belong to the Burial-Club."
              Chorus—Tol lol de rol, etc.

I arose up next morning at nine,
  Round my neck put my Sunday cravat;
To my boots gave a jolly good shine,
  In the water-pail dipped my silk hat.
Just a dollar I had to a cent;
  With brickdust I my cheeks gave a rub—
Then to the committee I went,
  And entered the Burial-Club.
                    Tol lol de rol, etc.

Then I sent my old woman one day
  (As a queer thought came into my head)
To the committee, and told her to say
  As how her poor husband was dead!

She went, and she pitched them a tale—
  With onions her eyes gave a rub;
So they gave her some cash on the nail,
  So we chiselled the Burial-Club.
                    Tol lol de rol, etc.

We next sent some notes to our friends,
  My wife and I shoved them about—
With "Mister John Johnson intends
  On giving a jolly blow-out!"
We'd a lot of pig's-feet and some bread,
  Six gallons of soup in a tub;
In fact, they were very well fed,
  At the expense of the Burial-Club!
                    Tol lol de rol, etc.

I served out the soup in good style,
  To show how genteel I had been;
And the old woman showed 'em, the while,
  How fast she could put away gin!
We ate one another, almost—
  And, after we'd finished the grub,
The old woman gave us a toast:
  "Here's long life to the Burial-Club!"
                    Tol lol de rol, etc.

We had a bass-fiddle and fife,
  A banjo, and cracked tambourine;
But, while dancing, I noticed my wife
  Steal off with a fellow called Green!
She told me, right bang to my head,
  She wished I'd been choked by the grub,
For she'd marry him when I was dead,
  With the blunt from the Burial-Club.
                    Tol lol de rol, etc.

We kept up the dancing all night,
  Till we couldn't dance any more;
And at last we were put in a fright,
  By a thundering knock at the door—

When a man in black popped in his head,
    Like the devil in search of his grub,
With "I've come for the man that's dead—
    I belong to the Burial-Club!"
                        Tol lol de rol, etc.

Our party rushed out of the room,
    After breaking the tables and chairs;
The old woman snatched up the broom,
    And knocked Mister Devil down-stairs!
We were both taken by the police,
    And locked up all night without grub;
And then got a twelvemonth apiece,
    For defrauding the Burial-Club!
                        Tol lol de rol, etc.

YACOB SCHNAPPS AND PEDER SCHPIKE.

A Parody on "Robin Ruff and Gaffer Green."

By JOHN F. POOLE.

YACOB SCHNAPPS.

IF I had but a dousand a year, Peder Schpike,
    If I had but a dousand a year,
Vot a veller I'd pe, un I'd have sooch a shpree,
    If I had but a dousand a year, Peder Schpike,
        If I had but *ein* dousand a year.

PEDER SCHPIKE.

Vot der tuyfel vas got in your head, Yacob Schnapps?
    You ish grazy as dunder, I fear!
But I'll listen mit you: dell me, vot vould you do,
    If you had but a dousand a year, Yacob Schnapps,
        If you had but *ein* dousand a year?

YACOB SCHNAPPS.

Vot I'd do? I'd puy lots of goot tings, Peder Schpike,
    Zwetzer-kaese, buddings, pretzels, un bier;
4*

I vould puild a pig house, have a couple of frows,
  If I had but a dousand a year, Peder Schpike,
  If I had but a dousand a year.

PEDER SCHPIKE.

But subbose you gets sick on your ped, Yacob Schnapps,
  Mit triuking too much lager-bier?
Un ven you grows old, if your frows 'gin to schold,
  Den vot ish your dousand a year, Yacob Schnapps,
  Den vot ish your dousand a year?

YACOB SCHNAPPS.

Vot, a man sich as me to get sick, Peder Schpike?
  I dinks dat vould pe butty queer:
Mine life I'd insure, un from Death pe secure,
  If I had but a dousand a year, Peder Schpike,
  If I had but a dousand a year.

PEDER SCHPIKE.

Dere's a place vot ish petter as dis, Yacob Schnapps.

YACOB SCHNAPPS.

Yaw, der shtate von New Yarsey ish near!

POTH TOGEDER.

Let us poth emigrate to dat peautifool shtate,
  Un ve'll soon make a dousand a year—yaw, inteed,
  Ve vill soon make a dousand a year!

THE INDIAN'S PRAYER.

LET me go to my home in the far distant land,
To the scenes of my childhood in innocence blest;
Where the tall cedars wave, and the bright waters flow
Where my fathers repose, let me go, let me go—
Where my fathers repose, let me go, let me go!

Let me go to the spot where the cataract plays,
Where oft I have sported in boyhood's bright days,
And greet my poor mother, whose heart will overflow
At the sight of her child: let me go, let me go—
At the sight of her child, let me go, let me go!

Let me go to my sire, by whose battle-scarred side
I have sported so oft in the morn of my pride,
And exulted to conquer the insolent foe:
To my father, the chief, let me go, let me go—
To my father, the chief, let me go, let me go!

And oh, let me go to my wild forest-home,
No more from its life-cheering pleasures to roam:
'Neath the groves of the glen let my ashes lie low;
To my home in the woods let me go, let me go—
To my home in the woods let me go, let me go!

OH, WHISTLE, AND I'LL COME TO YOU.

OH, whistle, and I'll come to you, my lad,
Oh, whistle, and I'll come to you, my lad;
Though father and mither and a' should go mad,
Oh, whistle, and I'll come to you, my lad!
But warily tent, when ye come to court me,
And come na unless the back-yett be a-jee;
Syne up the back stile, and let naebody see—
And come as ye were nae comin' to me—
Oh, come as ye were nae comin' to me!

Oh, whistle, and I'll come to you, my lad,
Oh, whistle, and I'll come to you, my lad;
Though father and mither and a' should go mad,
Thy Jeanie will venture wi' ye, my lad.
At kirk or at merket, whene'er ye meet me,
Gang by me as though ye cared nae a flie;
But steal me a blink o' your bonnie black e'e,
Yet look as ye were nae lookin' at me—
Oh, look as ye were nae lookin' at me!

THE HUMBUGGED HUSBAND.

Oh, whistle, and I'll come to you, my lad,
Oh, whistle, and I'll come to you, my lad;
Though father and mither and a' should go mad,
Oh, whistle, and I'll come to you, my lad!
Ay, vow and protest that ye care nae for me,
And whyles ye may lightly my beauty awee; .
But court nae anither, though jokin' ye be,
For fear that she wyle your fancy frae me—
For fear that she wyle your fancy frae me!

THE HUMBUGGED HUSBAND. (A Parody.)

As sung by the Hutchinson Family.

Air—"Alice Grey."

She's not what Fancy painted her—
  I'm sadly taken in;
If some one else had won her, I
  Should not have cared a pin!
I thought that she was mild and good
  As maiden e'er could be:
I wonder how she ever could
  Have so much humbugged me!

They cluster round and shake my hand,
  They tell me I am blest;
My case they do not understand—
  I think that I know best.
They call her "fairest of the fair,"
  They drive me mad and madder:
What do they mean by it?—I swear
  I only wish they had her!

'Tis true that she has lovely locks,
  That on her shoulders fall—
What would they say, to see the box
  In which she keeps them all?
Her taper fingers, it is true,
  Are difficult to match—
What would they say, if they but knew
  How terribly they scratch?

THE SAILOR-BOY'S GOOD-BY.

Air—"Woodman, spare that Tree."

My mother dear, I go
   Far o'er the distant sea—
But let me gladly know
   A blessing fond from thee.
The fate that makes us poor,
   Calls forth the parting sigh,
And drives me from thy door—
   My mother dear, good-by!

And when in distant lands
   I make my exiled prayer,
And raise my folded hands
   To Him who'll guide me there—
I'll crave for thee each joy,
   And He will hear my cry;
Then, smiling, kiss thy boy—
   My mother dear, good-by!

This poor but pretty cot,
   On which the sunset gleams,
Will ne'er be once forgot—
   'Twill mingle in my dreams.
And when from distant climes
   Thy truant boy comes nigh,
We'll share the happy times—
   My mother dear, good-by!

The thoughts of thy dear form,
   Thy cherished voice so kind,
Will cheer me in the storm,
   Amid the howling wind.
I dare not now remain;
   But quick the time will fly,
When we shall meet again—
   My mother dear, good-by!

ROOT, HOG, OR DIE.

I'M right from ole Virginny, wid my pocket full ob news;
I'm worth twenty shillings, right square in my shoes;
It doesn't make a dif of bitterence to neider you nor I,
Big pig or little pig—Root, hog, or die!

Chorus.

I'm chief cook and bottle-washer,
Cap'n ob de waiters;
I stand upon my head
When I peel de apple-dumplins!

I'se de happiest darkey on de top ob de earth;
I get fat as a 'possum in de time ob de dearth;
Like a pig in a 'tater-patch, dar let me lie,
'Way down in ole Virginny, whar it's Root, hog, or die!
I'm chief cook, etc.

De New York dandies dey look so very grand—
Ole clothes hand me down, gloves upon de hand,
High-heel-boots, mustaches round de eye,
A perfect sick family ob Root, hog, or die!
I'm chief cook, etc.

De New York gals dey do beat dem all;
Dey wear high-heel shoes for to make demselfs tall:
If dey don't hab dem, de Lor' how dey'll cry!
De boys hab got to get dem, or else Root, hog, or die!
I'm chief cook, etc.

De Shanghie coats dey're gettin' all de go—
Whar de boys get dem, I really don't know;
But dey're bound to get dem, if dey don't hang too high,
Or else dey make de tailors run, Root, hog, or die!
I'm chief cook, etc.

"I STAND upon the soil of freedom," cried a stump orator.
"No," exclaimed his shoemaker, "you stand in a pair of
boots that have never been paid for!"

DON GIOVANNI.

A Mysterious Melodrama,

Done into rhyme by W. T. MONCRIEFF.

AIR—"A Frog he would a wooing go."

THERE lived in Spain, as stories tell, oh,
  One Don Giovanni—
Among the girls a deuce of a fellow ;
And he had a servant they called Seporello,
  With his primo, buffo, canto, basso—
  "Heigho!" sighed Don Giovanni.

He serenaded Donna Anna,
  Did Don Giovanni ;
He swore she was more sweet than manna,
Then into her window he stole to trepan her,
  With his wheedle, tweedle, lango dillo—
  O wicked Don Giovanni !

The commandant, her guardian true,
  Caught Don Giovanni :
Says he, "You're a blackguard! run, sir, do"—
"I will," says Giovy, and run him through,
  With his carte-o, tierce-o, thrust-o, pierce-o,
  And away ran Don Giovanni.

He jumped in a boat, and was cast away—
  Wrecked Don Giovanni ;
Says he, "I shall keep the police here at bay,"   [pay,
Then some fishermen's *ribs* boned, and made their lives
  With his stop-'em, pop-'em, seize-'em, squeeze-'em—
  What a spark was Don Giovanni !

A wedding he met, and the bride 'gan to woo—
  Fie, Don Giovanni !
"I am running away, will you run away too?"
Says he.—"Yes," says she, "I don't care if I do"—
  With a helter-skelter, hesto, presto—
  What a devil was Don Giovanni !

To a churchyard he came—oh, what brought him there,
    Lost Don Giovanni?
The commandant's stone statue it made him stare,
Like Washington's statue at Union Square,
    With his saddle, bridle, falchion, truncheon—
    "Give me a call," said Don Giovanni.

To call on Giovanni the statue wasn't slow,
    Bold Don Giovanni.
"Will you sup with me, Mr. Statue?" said he. It cried, "No,
For you must sup with me in the regions below,
    Off my brimstone, sulphur, pitch-o, smoke-o!"—
    "I'll be d——d if I do!" cried Giovanni.

———

ANNIE LAURIE.

MAXWELLTON braes are bonnie,
    Where early fa's the dew,
And it's there that Annie Laurie
    Gi'ed me her promise true—
Gi'ed me her promise true,
    Which ne'er forgot will be,
And for bonnie Annie Laurie
    I'd lay me down and dee.

Her brow is like the snow-drift,
    Her neck is like the swan,
Her face it is the fairest
    That e'er the sun shone on—
That e'er the sun shone on,
    And dark blue is her e'e;
And for bonnie Annie Laurie, etc.

Like dew on the gowan lying,
    Is the fa' o' her fairy feet;
And like winds in summer sighing,
    Her voice is low and sweet—
Her voice is low and sweet,
    And she's a' the world to me:
And for bonnie Annie Laurie, etc.

RORY O'MORE.

YOUNG Rory O'More courted Kathaleen Bawn—
He was bold as a hawk, and she soft as the dawn;
He wished in his heart pretty Kathaleen to please,
And he thought the best way to do that was to tease.
"Now, Rory, be aisy," sweet Kathaleen would cry,
Reproof on her lip, but the smile in her eye;
"With your tricks, I don't know in truth what I'm about;
Faith, you've teased till I've put on my cloak inside out."
"O jewel," says Rory, "that same is the way
You've thrated my heart for this many a day;
And 'tis plazed that I am, and why not, to be sure?
For 'tis all for good luck," says bold Rory O'More.

"Indeed, then," says Kathaleen, "don't think of the like,
For I half gave a promise to soothering Mike;
The ground that I walk on he loves, I'll be bound."
"Faith," says Rory, "I'd rather love you than the ground."
"Now, Rory, I'll cry, if you don't let me go;
Sure I dream every night that I'm hating you so."
"Oh!" says Rory, "that same I'm delighted to hear,
For dhrames always go by conthraries, my dear;
O jewel, keep dhraming that same till you die,
And Morning will give dirty Night the black lie;
And 'tis plazed that I am, and why not, to be sure?
Since 'tis all for good luck," says bold Rory O'More.

"Arrah, Kathaleen, my darling, you've teased me enough,
And I've thrashed, for your sake, Dinny Grimes and Jim Duff;
And I've made myself, drinking your health, quite a baste;
So I think, after that, I may talk to the praste."
Then Rory, the rogue, stole his arms round her neck—
So soft and so white, without freckle or speck—
And he looked in her eyes, that were beaming with light,
And he kissed her sweet lips, don't you think he was right?
"Now, Rory, leave off, sir! you'll hug me no more—
That's eight times to-day that you've kissed me before."
"Then here goes another," says he, "to make sure,
For there's luck in odd numbers," says Rory O'More.

5

THE FINE OULD IRISH GINTLEMAN.

I'll sing you a fine ould song, made by a find ould Paddy's
  pate,
Of a fine ould Irish gintleman, who had the divil a taste of
  an estate,
Except a fine ould patch of pitatys that he liked exceed-
  ingly to ate,   '
For they were beef to him, and mutton too, and barring a
  · red herring or a rusty rasher of bacon now and thin,
  almost every other sort of mate;
Yet this fine ould Irish gintleman was one of the rale ould
  stock!

His cabin-walls were covered o'er with fine ould Irish mud
Because he couldn't afford to have any paper hangings, and
  between you and me he wouldn't give a pin for them
  if he could;
And jist as proud as Julius Sayzer, or Alixander the Great,
  this independent ragamuffin stood,
With a glass of fine ould Irish whiskey in his fist, which
  , he's decidedly of opinion will do a mighty dale of
  good,
To this fine ould Irish gintleman, all of the rale ould stock!

Now this fine ould Irish gintleman wore mighty curious
  clothes—
Though, for comfort, I'll be bail that they'd bate any of
  your fashionable beaux;
For when the sun was very hot, the gintle wind right
  through his ventilation garments most beautifully
  blows;
And he's never troubled with any corns, and I'll tell you
  why—because he despises the wakeness of wearing
  any thing as hard as leather on his toes;
Yet this fine ould Irish gintleman was one of the rale ould
  stock!

Now this fine ould Irish gintleman has a mighty curious
  knack

Of flourishing a tremendous great shillaly in his hand, and
    letting it drop down with a most uncompromising.
    whack ;
So, of most superior shindies, you may take your oath, if
    you ever happen to be called upon, for it he very
    nearly never had a lack ;
And it's very natural, and not at all surprising, to suppose
    that the fine ould Irish mud was well acquainted
    with the back
Of this fine ould Irish gintleman, all of the rale ould stock!

This fine ould Irish gintleman he was once out upon a
    spree,
And, as many a fine ould Irish gintleman has done, and
    more betoken will do to the end of time, he got
    about as dhrunk as he could be ;
His senses was completely mulvathered, and the conse-
    quence was that he could neither hear nor see ;
So they thought he was stone dead and gone intirely—so
    the best thing they could do would be to have him
    waked and buried dacintly,
Like a fine ould Irish gintleman, all of the rale ould stock ! ·

So this fine ould Irish gintleman he was laid out upon a
    bed,
With half a dozen candles at his heels, and two or three
    dozen, more or less, about his head ;
· But when the whiskey-bottle was uncorked, he couldn't
    stand it any longer, so he riz right up in bed—
"And when sich mighty fine stuff as that is going about,"
    says he, "ye don't think I'd be sich a soft-headed
    fool as to be dead?"
Oh, this fine ould Irish gintleman it was mighty hard to
    kill !

"Pat, is it a son or a daughter that your sister has
got ?"
    "Faith, I don't yet know whether I am an uncle or an
aunt."

PRAYER-BOOKS AND CORKSCREWS.

A Song with a Moral.

AIR—"Derry down."

TWELVE parsons once went to a 'Squire's to dine,
Who was famous for giving good ven'son and wine;
All great friends of the *cloth*, with good living in view,
Quite *grace-full* they sat down, as parsons should do.
Chorus—Derry down, etc.

A wicked young whipster, our worthy 'Squire's cousin,
Whispered, "Cousin, I boldly will lay you a dozen,
Though here we've a dozen of parsons, God wot,
Not one of the twelve has a prayer-book got!"
Derry down, etc.

"Agreed!" cried the 'Squire; "coz, we must not be loth
Such a wager to lay, for the sake of the cloth;
The parsons, no doubt, to confute you are able,
So we'll bring, with the dinner, the bet on the table."
Derry down, etc.

Dinner came—cried the 'Squire, "A new grace I will say;
Has any one here got a prayer-book, pray?"
Quite glum looked the parsons, and with one accord
Cried, "Mine's lost"—"Mine's at home"—"Mine's at church,
by the Lord!"   Derry down, etc.

Quoth our cousin, "Dear 'Squire, I my wager have won,
But another I purpose to win ere I've done:
Though the parsons could not bring a prayer-book to view,
I the same bet will lay they have each a corkscrew!"
Derry down, etc.

"Done—done!" roared the 'Squire.—"Hello, butler! bring
nearer
That excellent magnum of ancient Madeira."

'Twas brought.—"Let's decant it—a corkscrew, good
   John."
Here each of the parsons roared out, "I've got one!"
                    Derry down, etc.

MORAL.

But let us not censure our parsons for this—
When a thing's in its place, it can ne'er come amiss:
Prayer-books won't serve for corkscrews; and I'm such a
   sinner,
Though a sermon I like, I don't want it at dinner.
                    Derry down, etc.

JANE O'MALLEY.

I'LL tell thee a tale of a maiden's veil,
   It was worn by Jane O'Malley;
On the Highland green her form was seen,
   But she now sleeps in the valley!
      Chorus—She now sleeps,
            She now sleeps in the valley.

One year ago, when the sun was low,
   Along with Elwyn Ally,
To chat and talk, she took a walk—
   But she now sleeps in the valley!
            She now sleeps, etc.

They talked of love—she stood above
   A rocky cliff, with Ally:
Alas! she fell—he could not save—
   And she now sleeps in the valley!
            She now sleeps, etc.

They searched the ground till the spot was found,
   Where struggled Jane O'Malley—
Where the rock was cleft, her veil was left,
   And she now sleeps in the valley!
            She now sleeps, etc.

5*

LODGINGS IN PAT McGARADIE'S.

A Rollicking Irish Song.

Sung by FRED MAY.

AIR—"Barney McFinnegan."

SOME folks know the way for to thrive,
   In spite of the world's adversity—
And enjoy all the good things alive,
   When others are dying from scarcity.
Two Paddies, I very well know,
   They made of misfortune a paradise;
They came from sweet Donoghaloo,
   And took lodgings in Pat McGaradie's.
               Chorus—Whack, fol de rol, etc.

Now they spoke to a grocer hard by,
   And prevailed on the man for to tick 'em;
But the payment was "all in my eye,"
   For the rascals intended for to trick him.
So they ate as they ne'er did before,
   And smacked their lips wid the rarities—
Saying, "Mate and drink in the store,
   And lodgings in Pat McGaradie's!"
               Whack, fol de rol, etc.

They brought in every night, to their pad,
   The boys just come o'er to the shearing;
Be the hokey! and that was the squad
   That could give the victuals a tearing!
"Fire away, lads! there's plenty o' more—
   Taste your lips wid the rarities;
There's mate and dhrink in the store,
   And lodgings in Pat McGaradie's!"
               Whack, fol de rol, etc.

Sure, they made knives of their fists
   (For there's many a rule in the navy),
And Paddy was up to the wrists,
   Dealing them handfuls of gravy!

"Slash away, till your bellies are sore—
Show them your ateing dexterities!
There's mate and dhrink in the store,
And lodgings in Pat McGaradie's!"
                    Whack, fol de rol, etc.

The porter and ale were marked "tay,"
And the whiskey "spice" and "onions;"
And they cried, "Let us all tear away,
And give our stomachs new linings!
Such luck niver happened before—
Fill up yer cups wid the rarities;
There's mate and dhrink in the store,
And lodgings in Pat McGaradie's!"
                    Whack, fol de rol, etc.

The dogs, from all quarters around,
Were never before so befriended;
And while the good things did abound,
The beggars were duly attended.
"Now let us be kind to the poor,
And we'll get a good name for our charities;
There's mate and dhrink in the store,
And lodgings in Pat McGaradie's!"
                    Whack, fol de rol, etc.

But, the grocer's account being due,
He asked for his money quite civil,
And was tould by the beggarly crew
To go and seek that from the divil!
With rage how he cursed and he swore!
They had ruined him ateing his rarities:
He turned bankrupt, and shut up his store,
Through those doings at Pat McGaradie's.
                    Whack, fol de rol, etc.

—————

IF a fellow has but one eye, let him get a wife, and she
will be his other I.

THE BANKS OF CLAUDY.

IT was on a summer's morning, all in the.month of May,
Down by yon flowery garden, where Betsey did stray;
I overheard a damsel in sorrow to complain,
All for her absent lover, that ploughs the raging main.

I went up to this fair maid, and put her in surprise;
I own she did not know me, I being in disguise.
Said I, "My charming creature, my joy and heart's delight,
How far do you travel this dark and rainy night?"

"The way, kind sir, to Claudy, if you please to show—
Pity a maid distracted, for there I have to go!
I am in search of a faithless young man, Johnny is his name,
All on the banks of Claudy I am told he does remain.

"If Johnny was here this night, he would keep me from all
        harm—
He is in the field of battle, all in his uniform:
As he's in the field of battle, his foes he will destroy—
Like a ruling king of honor, he fought in the wars of Troy."

"It's six weeks and better since your true-love left the
        shore;
He's cruising the wide ocean, where foaming billows roar·
He's cruising the wild ocean, for honor and gain—
I was told the ship was wrecked off the coast of Spain."

When she heard the dreadful news, she fell, in despair,
To wringing of her hands and tearing of her hair.
"Since he is gone and left me, no man will I take;
In some lonesome valley I will wander for his sake!"

His heart was filled with joy—no longer could he stand;
He flew into her arms, saying, "Betsey, I am the man—
I am the faithless young man whom you thought was slain,
And, since we're met on Claudy's banks, we'll never part
        again."

SALL BRILL AND SQUINTING WILL.

A Simple little Ditty.

AIR—"The Girl I left behind me."

I LOVED a girl called Pretty Sal,
  In courtship so particular—
Just three feet high, she'd but one eye,
  Her breath was like the auricula.
Her flaxen pate and waddling gait
  Did seem so like divinity—
So sweet her leer, I cried, "Oh, dear,
  I'll love you for infinity!"

I sent her word, on a fine card,
  With figures emblematical,
That I would come and take her home—
  In that I was dogmatical!
But she said, "No! if I said so
  From now to all infinity,
That I should find it was her mind
  With me to have no affinity!"

One day, oh dear! as you shall hear,
  By my own incongruity,
I met Sal Brill with Squinting Will,
  In closest contiguity.
Oh, then she said, "Sweet Will I'll wed,
  To end all ambiguity;
Gibby, good-by! you're 'all my eye'—
  We'll live in continuity."

FLOW GENTLY, SWEET AFTON.

FLOW gently, sweet Afton, among thy green braes;
Flow gently—I'll sing thee a song in thy praise;
My Mary's asleep by thy murmuring stream;
Flow gently, sweet Afton, disturb not her dream.

-Thou dove, whose soft echo resounds from the hill!
Thou green-crested lapwing, with noise loud and shrill!
Ye wild whistling warblers! your music forbear!
I charge you disturb not the slumbering fair.

Thy crystal stream, Afton, how lovely it glides,
And winds by the cot where my Mary resides!
There oft, as mild evening weeps over the lea,
Thy sweet-scented groves shade my Mary and me.
Flow gently, sweet Afton, among thy green braes;
Flow gently, sweet river, the theme of my lays;
My Mary's asleep by thy murmuring stream—
Flow gently, sweet Afton, disturb not her dream.

THE LANDLADY OF FRANCE.

A Rare Old Comic Song.

AIR—"Yankee Doodle."

A LANDLADY of France loved an officer, 'tis said,
And this officer he dearly loved her brandy, oh.
Sighed she, "I love this officer, although his nose is red,
And his legs are what his regiment call bandy, oh."

But when the bandy officer was ordered to the coast,
How she tore her lovely locks, that looked so sandy, oh!
"Adieu, my soul!" said she; "if you write, pray pay the
    post—
And, before we part, let's take a drop of brandy, oh."

She filled him out a bumper just before he left the town,
And another for herself so neat and handy, oh;
So they kept their spirits up by pouring spirits down,
For love is like the colic, cured with brandy, oh.

"Take a bottle on't," says she, "for you're going into camp;
In your tent, you know, my love, 'twill be the dandy, oh."
"You're right, my love," says he, "for a tent is very damp,
And 'tis better with my tent to take some brandy, oh."

THE HAZEL-DELL.

(By permission of the publishers, Messrs. W. HALL & SON.)

In the Hazel-Dell my Nelly's sleeping—
Nelly, loved so long!
And my lonely, lonely watch I'm keeping,
Nelly lost and gone.
Here in moonlight often we have wandered
Through the silent shade;
Now where leafy branches drooping downward,
Little Nelly's laid.

Chorus.

All alone my watch I'm keeping,
In the Hazel-Dell;
For my darling Nelly's near me sleeping—
Nelly, dear, farewell!

In the Hazel-Dell my Nelly's sleeping,
Where the flowers wave;
And the silent stars are nightly weeping
O'er poor Nelly's grave.
Hopes that once my bosom fondly cherished,
Smile no more on me;
Every dream of joy, alas! has perished,
Nelly, dear, with thee.

All alone my watch, etc.

Now I'm weary, friendless, and forsaken,
Watching here alone;
Nelly, thou no more wilt fondly cheer me
With thy loving tone.
Yet forever shall thy gentle image
In my memory dwell;
And my tears thy lonely grave shall moisten—
Nelly, dear, farewell!

All alone my watch, etc.

I'LL BE NO SUBMISSIVE WIFE.

I'LL be no submissive wife,
　　No, not I—no, not I;
I'll not be a slave for life,
　　No, not I—no, not I:
I'll be no submissive wife,
　　No, not I—no, not I;
I'll not be a slave for life,
　　No, not I—no, not I !
Think you, on a wedding-day,
That I said, as others say,
"Love, and honor, and obey—
Love, and honor, and obey"?
No, no, no, no, no, no, no, no, no, not I !

Chorus.
"Love, and honor, and obey—
Love, and honor, and obey"?
No, no, no, no, no, no, no, no, no, not I;
No, no, no, no, no, no, no, no, no, not I;
No, no, no, no, no, no, no, no, no, no, not I !

I to dulness don't incline,
　　No, not I—no, not I;
Go to bed at half-past nine?
　　No, not I—no, not I !
I to dulness don't incline,
　　No, not I—no, not I;
Go to bed at half-past nine?
　　No, not I—no, not I !
Should a humdrum husband say
That at home I ought to stay,
Do you think that I'll obey—
Do you think that I'll obey?
No, no, no, no, no, no, no, no, no, not I;
Do you think that I'll obey—
Do you think that I'll obey?
No, no, no, no, no, no, no, no, no, not I;
No, no, no, no, etc.

NO! NO!

The celebrated Duett in the Burletta of "No."

As sung by JAMES DUNN and Mrs. W. G. JONES, at the New Bowery Theatre.

AIR—"Isabel."

HE. Will you not bless, with one sentence, a lover
Whose bosom beats only for you?
The cause of your anger I pr'ythee discover—
Pray tell me the reason for?

SHE. No!

HE. Say, dearest, you still love me?

SHE. No!

HE. Oh, how can you doom me to sorrow?
Yet once again bless me with—

SHE. No!

HE. And promise to meet me to-morrow:
Promise—

SHE. No!

HE. Pr'ythee—

SHE. No!

HE. Don't say no!

HE. Must we, then, dearest Maria, sever?
And can you, then, part with me?·

SHE. No!

HE. Then swear by yon sun to be mine only ever;
You cannot refuse me, love!

SHE. No!

HE. You hate not your fond lover?

SHE. No!

HE. Your hand to my faithful heart pressing,
Say, does it offend you, love?

No!

HE. Then to marry will not be distressing—
Answer!

SHE. No!

HE. Once more.

SHE. No! no! no! no!

6

BACHELOR BARNEY O'NEIL.

Sung by WILLIAM W. REEVE, comedian and comic vocalist, at the
Theatres and Music-Halls.

AIR—"Oh, dear, what can the matter be?"

OCH, botheration! Miss Judy O'Flanagan,
Give me my heart back, and make me a man agin;
Such a conflict of passions I niver can stand agin—
  Och, blur an' ouns! what can I ail?
My legs do so trimble, my teeth do so chatter;
My heart is as soft as a basin of batter;
Och, gramachree! what the divil's the matter .
  With poor Misther Barney O'Neil?

One evening alone in the fields I did meet her—
"Och, Judy," thinks I, "yer a swate, lovely craiture."
Her cheeks were as round as a maily potatur,
  Her step airy, light, and ginteel.
Her glance was as keen as a dart or an arrow;
In one moment it shot me right plump to the marrow,
And I felt like a rattlesnake in a wheelbarrow—
  Faix, it bothered poor Barney O'Neil!

Now after a twelvemonth of coortship I'd tarried,
I bothered her so to consent to be married:
She gave it, and quickly was to the priest carried,
  And I there made her Misthress O'Neil.
Our neighbors and frinds were all merry and frisky,
And, afther partaking of lashings of whiskey,
They bade us adieu, wishing joy to us briskly,
  And a young Misther Barney O'Neil!

By night and by day did I swear I did love her,
While she swately promised she'd ne'er prove a rover;
But the honeymoon scarcely a week had passed over,
  When a divil was Misthress O'Neil!
At clawing, och! faith, not a woman could bate her;
And thin, as to tongue, she'd the divil's own clatter;
Och, sure, but I soon wondered what was the matter
  With poor Misther Barney O'Neil.

One evening, och! surely Ould Nick wouldn't match her,
Returnin' home airly, I happened to catch her
Wid her arms round the neck of a tall sarjint-major—
    Och, blur an' ouns, how I did feel! ·
Of Judy's foul parjury I did remind her,
And bundled the major quick out of the winder;
Manewhile, like a furnace, or blazing-hot cinder,
    Burnt poor Misther Barney O'Neil.

Next mornin' the major was kilt in a dhuel;
Judy bewept him, and called the Fates cruel—
Fell sick of a fever, and died of hot gruel—
    Death quieted Misthress O'Neil.
I miss her, because she no longer can taize me;
No longer I roam like a man that is crazy,
So the rest of me life I'll spind parfectly aisy,
    Will Bachelor Barney O'Neil.

THE GAY LITTLE POSTMAN.

An Old-Style Comic Song.

As sung by all the comic vocalists.

Air—"Mr. Walker."

But a short way up-town, though I mustn't tell where,
A shoemaker married a maiden so fair,
Who a month after wedlock, 'tis truth I declare,
    Fell in love with a gay little postman.

Her person was thin, genteel, and tall,
Her carroty hair did in ringlets fall;
And while the cobbler worked hard at his stall,
    She was watching this gay little postman.

He was just four feet six in height,
But a well-made figure to the sight;
He walked like a monument bolt upright—
    Mr. Walker, the gay little postman.

His toes he turned out; he had bright black eyes;
His nose was more than the common size,
And he really looked, without any lies,
  Too genteel and neat for a postman.

Resolved she was to get in his way:
So, without any trouble, she met him one day,
And says she, "Have you got e'er a letter, I say,
  For me, Mister gay little postman?"

Says he, "I don't know you." Says she, "Good lack
I live the next door, the second floor back;
My husband's a cobbler—'tis all in your track."
  "It's all right," says the gay little postman,

Next morning—I can't tell you what she was at—
She felt her heart suddenly beat pit-a-pat,
When she heard at the street-door a double "Rat-tat!"
  And in came the gay little postman.

"Here's a letter," says he—the cunning elf!—
"The postage is paid—so't needs no pelf."
In fact, he had written the letter himself,
  And brought it, the gay little postman!

With love in his eyes he then at her did stare;
Says he, "I ne'er saw a lady so fair;
I always was partial to carroty hair—
  was," says the gay little postman.

"That your husband ill treats you I can't suppose"—
"Yes, he gives me bad words, and sometimes blows;
He's an ugly man, and has got no nose"—
  "I have!" says the gay little postman.

His kindness was such, that it knew no end;
And to prove that he really was a true friend,
He took her spouse three pair of shoes to mend—
  Did Walker, the gay little postman.

They were soled and heeled without delay;
To the cobbler he had so much to say,
He got the shoes, but as for the pay—
    "Chalk it down," says the gay little postman.

Ever since then, they've led a cat-and-dog life;
Their home, bed, and board have been nothing but strife;
The cobbler was "done," and so was his wife,
    By Walker, the gay little postman:

For, by way of a finish to this vile act,
The lady (depend on't, 'tis a fact)
Has brought him a boy, the image exact
    Of Walker, the gay little postman!

MEET ME, MISS MOLLY MALONE,

A Parody on "Meet Me by Moonlight alone."

Sung by Geo. C. Edeson, comedian and vocalist.

Meet me, Miss Molly Malone,
    In the grove at the end of the vale;
But be sure you don't come there alone—
    Bring a pot of your master's strong ale,
With a nice bit of beef and some bread;
    Some pickles, or cucumbers green,
Or a nice little dainty pig's head—
    'Tis the loveliest tit-bit e'er seen.
                Then meet me, etc.

Pastry may do for the gay,
    Old maids may find comfort in tea;
But there's something about ham and beef
    That agrees a deal better with me.
Remember my cupboard is bare—
    Then come, if my dear life you prize;
I'd have lived the last fortnight on air,
    But you sent me two nice mutton-pies!
                Then meet me, etc,

6*

DOCTOR O'TOOLE,
And his Illigant School.

As sung by ED BERRY, comedian and vocalist.

AIR—"Derry down."

IN this wonderful age, when most men go to college,
And every man's head has a hatful of knowledge,
'Twill soon be a wonder to meet with a fool,
When such men are abroad as Professor O'Toole—
       Great Doctor O'Toole, and his illigant school.

There are very few men, like O'Toole, who can teach:
If the head won't respond, he applies to the breech!
And whacking them well, till with blows they are full,
"Let's knock in the larnin'!" says Doctor O'Toole.
       Great Doctor O'Toole, etc.

One morning, the Doctor went out to his walk,
And he saw on the door his own portrait in chalk:
That morning he flogged every boy in the school!—
"It's a part of my system," says Doctor O'Toole.
       Great Doctor O'Toole, etc.

"Get on with your lessons as fast as you can,
For knowledge is sweeter than eggs and fried ham;
Don't try to deceive me, like ducks in a pool,
Or I'll blow you to blazes!" says Doctor O'Toole.
       Great Doctor O'Toole, etc.

"And now, my dear children, bear always in mind
That words without meaning are nothing but wind;
Accept of all favors, make that the first rule,
Or you're a parcel of asses!" says Doctor O'Toole.
       Great Doctor O'Toole, etc.

"If you go to a house, and they ask you to eat,
Don't hold your head down, and refuse the good meat;
But say you will drink too, or, just like the mule,
You're unworthy of lessons from Doctor O'Toole."
       Great Doctor O'Toole, etc.

"When your father and mother have turned their backs
Don't kick up a row with the dogs and the cats;
Nor tie the pig's tail to the table or stool,
For you're a parcel of divils!" says Doctor O'Toole.
　　　　　Great Doctor O'Toole, etc.

"But give over fightin', and think of your sins,
Or I'll break every bone in your impudent skins!
Give over your ructions, don't think me a fool,
Or I'll punish you blackguards!" says Doctor O'Toole.
　　　　　Great Doctor O'Toole, etc.

"Now the lessons are over, so run away home;
Don't turn up your nose at a crust or a bone:
Come back in the morning, for that is the rule,
And you'll get more instruction from Doctor O'Toole."
　　　　　Great Doctor O'Toole, etc.

HIGGINS'S BALL.

An Irish Narrative in Rhyme.

As sung by FRED MAY.

AIR—"Paddy O'Carroll."

ARRAH, haven't you heard of Higgins's ball,
Where Fashion's devotees so gay mustered all?
If not, and you'll listen to what I describe,
It's the joys of a trip to this musical tribe.
There was wealthy ould citizens there, d'ye see—
The boys and the girls dressed as fine as could be,
And some out-and-out buffers, a dozen in all,
We made up our minds for a trip to the ball.

Chorus.

There was Barney O'Fagan and Timothy Hagan,
　　Miss Molly McGuffin and Judy McCall;
Aunts, uncles, and cousins, and neighbors by dozens,
　　All welting the flure at ould Higgins's ball.

Now, whin ready to start, how the people did stare!
We had aich of us got something patent and rare;
We made up our minds we the nation would stun,
And arrived just in time as the ball had begun.
There ould Higgins we saw in his new patent boots—
(*Spoken.*) Bad luck to him! sure, his ould father, Barney
 Higgins, niver wore any thing but brogues—
Quite busy a-tunin' the fiddles and flutes;
And a group of musicians, all of the right sort,
Whose noise and whose whims fill the room full of sport.
       There was, etc.

Now the time had arrived for the ball to begin,
And the music struck up such a terrible din!
Wid ould Misthress H. at the top o' the dance,
Each merry young couple did quickly advance.
Och! thin, what wid treadin' on aich other's toes,
And knockin' our heads against many a nose,
Kickin' aich other's ankles, we welted the flure,
While Higgins kept time wid the bar of the dure.
(*Spoken, by ould Higgins.*) Hurroo! lively, b'yes! See
 here, Patsey Molloy, if I catch you steppin' on the
 girls' skirts, I declare to my conscience I'll give you a
 welt across the head wid the bar of the dure!
       There was, etc,

Now things went on well till McGinniss the snob
From me my young woman was tryin' to rob;
Arrah, thin such a terrible fight did ensue!
And the rest joinin' in, at aich other they flew.
Peggy Murphy called Higgins "an ould drunken sot"—
(*Spoken.*) Divil's cure to him, so he was! He'd dhrink
 the Atlanthic Say dhry, if it was built of whiskey—
Whin away at her head flew the big pratee-pot!
My valor, for Peggy, I very soon shows,
Jist by breakin' the bridge of ould Higgins's nose.
(*Spoken.*) Sarves him right, the dirty blaggard!
       There was, etc.

Now they all left the place in such a terrible mess,
All covered with portions of bonnets and dress,
Until, quite exhausted, they all fell asleep,
And there next mornin' they all lay in a heap!
(*Spoken.*) The dhrunken bastes, to sleep in their clothes,
  like pigs!
Now if ever I venture to go there again,
There's one thing I'll tell, and that's mighty plain—
I'll not forget soon, faix! if ever at all,
The illigant fight we'd at Higgins's ball.

There was, etc.

PARODY ON "MOTHER, I'VE COME HOME TO DIE."

An Original Conglomeration of Titles.

By E. T. JOHNSTON.

DEAR mother, I remember well
  "That nice young gal from New Jersey;"
She said, "Oh kiss, but never tell!"
  "How are you, black-horse cavalry?"
"Then let me like a soldier fall,"
  "When the swallows homeward fly;"
"Come, landlord, fill the flowing bowl"—
  "Dear mother, I've come home to die."

Chorus.

"Call me pet names," "Annie Lisle,"
  "A bully boy with a glass eye;"
"Oh, let her rip! she's all O. K."—
  "Dear mother, I've come home to die."

"Oh, hark! I hear an angel sing"
  "I'll be free and easy still!"
"My love he is a sailor-boy,"
  With "The sword of Bunker Hill."

Oh, "Happy, happy be thy dreams,"
  When you're "Comin' thro' the rye;"
"I wish I was in Dixie's Land"—
  "Dear mother, I've come home to die."
             Call me, etc.

"Dear Tom," "'Twas my grandma's advice,"
  "Don't ever fly your kite too high;"
"I'm over young to marry yet,"
  "Says the spider to the fly."
"We met by chance," at "Donnybrook Fair,"
  Where "No Irish need apply;"
"I dreamt I dwelt in marble halls"—
  "Dear mother, I've come home to die."
             Call me, etc.

"Yes, dearest, I will love thee more,"
  "I'll hang my harp on a willow-tree;"
"Our Billy was a butcher-boy,"
  And "Sally is the gal for me."
"A dainty plant's the Ivy green,"
  "Then, comrades, raise your banners high;"
"I wish I had a fat contract"—
  "Dear mother, I've come home to die."
             Call me, etc.

SNIGSBY keeps a diary since it has become fashionable. Being in a poetical mood the other evening, he made the following entry, which may serve as a pattern to the afflicted:

    "A nuther day is past and gon
    Bill Jinkins broke my demmy gon
    I'm turnin' in at half-past six
    The moon's a dumplin', fiddle stix."

WHAT is the apparent difference between the Prince of Wales, an orphan, a bald head, and a gorilla? The Prince of Wales is the heir apparent, an orphan has no'er a parent, a bald head has no hair apparent, and a gorilla has a hairy parent.

SOCIAL SENTIMENTS;

OR,

Toasts for all Times.

A COBWEB pair of breeches, a porcupine saddle, a hard-trotting horse, and a long journey, to the enemies of freedom and progress!

Firmness in the senate, valor in the field, and fortitude on the waves.

Cork to the heels, cash to the pockets, courage to the hearts, and concord to the heads, of the soldiers of freedom.

Improvement to our arts, and invention to our artists.

May the Tree of Liberty flourish around the globe, and every human being partake of its fruits!

May the skins of our foes be turned into parchment, and our rights written thereon.

The three great Generals in power—General Peace, General Plenty, and General Satisfaction.

America's emblem, our glorious eagle,
  Who seeks to destroy him, forever shall fail,
If they think that proud bird they can ever inveigle
  By sprinkling salt on his venerable tail!

May the boat of Pleasure always be steered by the pilot of Reason.

  A drop of good-stuff, and a pleasant party,
  To spend the evening social and hearty.

May the freedom of election be preserved, the trial by jury maintained, and the liberty of the press secured, to the latest posterity.

The inside of a house, and the outside of a prison.

May he who betrays his country, know the want of a country to shelter in.

  May the juice of the rich grape enliven each soul,
  And Good-Humor preside at the head of each bowl;
  We meet to be merry, then let us part wise,
  Nor suffer the bottle to blind Reason's eyes.

May the devil never pay visits abroad, nor receive company at home!

May Fortune fill the cup when Charity guides the hand.

Great men honest, and honest men great.

A pot and a pipe, and a good-natured wife,
Just to make me feel happy the rest of my life.

Short shoes and long corns to our country's enemies.

Champagne to our real friends, and real pain to our sham friends.

Friendship in marble, animosity in dust.

Envy in an air-pump, without a passage to breathe through.

May every honest man *turn out* a rogue.

Lenity to the faults of others, and sense to discover our own.

Health of body, peace of mind, a clean shirt, and a dollar in our pocket.

Here's to Columbia, the hope of the world!
Long may her navy, triumphantly sailing,
And army still conquer with courage unfailing,
Their thunder forever 'gainst tyrants be hurled!

Here's to the man that raised the goose that gave the quill that made the pen that signed the Declaration of Independence !

May our laws guard our liberty, and our liberty our laws.

Let the hoary miser toil,
We such sordid views despise;
Give us wine and Beauty's smile,
There each glowing rapture lies.

Addition to our trade, multiplication to our manufactures, subtraction to our taxes, and reduction to useless offices.

All Fortune's daughters, except the eldest Mis-Fortune.

THE END.

MOORE'S IRISH MELODIES.

TONY PASTOR'S "OWN" COMIC VOCALIST.

TONY PASTOR'S IRISH COMIC SONGSTER.

THE HEART AND HOME SONGSTER.

THE DONNYBROOK FAIR COMIC SONGSTER.

THE CAMP-FIRE SONG BOOK.

TONY PASTOR'S UNION SONG BOOK.

TONY PASTOR'S COMIC SONGSTER.

FLORENCES' IRISH BOY AND YANKEE GIRL SONGSTER.

BOB HART'S PLANTATION SONGSTER,

Contents of Dick & Fitzgerald's Dime Song Books.   5

THE LOVE AND SENTIMENTAL SONGSTER.

A Penny for your Thoughts
Alice Gray
Autumn Leaves be Strewed
Aggie Asthore
All's for the Best
Brightest Eves
Be Off with You, Now
Ben Bolt
Beautiful Silver Sea
Come Into the Garden, Maud
Evening Star
Ever of Thee
Emma Lee
Ellen Bayne
Good News from Home
Good Night! Beloved
Good-Bye, Sweetheart!
Give Me a Cot in the Valley
Home Again
Hark, I Hear an Angel Sing
He Doeth all Things Well
I Ask but for One Thrilling Kiss
I Wandered by the Brook-side
I am Leaving Thee
I'd Offer Thee this Hand
I'm Not Myself at All
In this Old Chair
Jenny's Coming o'er the Green
Kitty Tyrrell

Kathleen Mavourneen
Katy Darling
Kitty of Coleraine
Little Jenny Dow
Lizzie Dies To-Night
Listen to the Mocking Bird
Last Greeting
Let the Toast be Dear Woman
Love Me Little Love Me Long
Mary Aileen
Molly Bawn
My Mother Dear
My Soul In One Unbroken Sigh
Mary of Argyle
Norah, the Pride of Kildare
Norah McShane
Norah, Darling, Don't Believe Them
Oh, Where's the Harm of a Little Kiss
Pretty Jane
Rock Me to Sleep, Mother
Rocked in the Cradle
Shells of Ocean
Scenes that are Brightest
Some One to Love
The Dearest Spot
The Gambler's Wife
The Silver Moon
The Dying Californian
The Low-backed Car
The Heart Bowed Down

The Standard Bearer
The Irish Emigrant's Lament
The Harp that Once
The Pirate's Serenade
The Ivy Green
The Light of Other Days
The Good-bye at the Door
The Dreams of the Heart
The Miller's Daughter
The Murmuring Sea
The Three Ages of Love
Then You'll Remember Me
Thou Art Gone from my Gaze
Thou Art Mine Own, Love
'Tis Midnight Hour
True Friendship
Twilight Dews
'Tis Hard to Give the Hand
Where the Heart can Never Be Gone
Why Have My Loved Ones When the Swallows Homeward Fly
Where are the Friends
Would I Were a Boy Again
We Met by Chance
Why Do I Love Thee Yet
Within a Mile of Edinboro' Town
Will You Love Me Then as Now

FRANK BROWER'S BLACK DIAMOND SONGSTER.

A Darkey's Epitaph
A Dutchman's Opinion of Things Now-a-Days
A Joke on Smoke
A Lazy Wife
Altogether too Clean
A Modest Request
A Tough Boarding House
A Very Deaf Darkey
Ben Battle and Nellie Gray
Black and Blue
Blow Your Horn, Gabriel
Bully Boy's the Butterfly
Burlesque Oration on Matrimony
Come Down wid de Brass
Cry and Color
De Cappy Lan I of Hannan
De Milk in de Cocoa-Nut
De Mysterious Knockings
De Ole Plantation
Filibuster Sam

Frank Brower's New Medley
Happy Uncle Tom
Hoolagan McCarthy
How to Get up a Concert
I Wish I Had a Fat Contract
Johnny Succotash
Kit the Cobbler
Marriage Bliss
Model Rhymes
New "Cum Plung Cum"
Nigger Under de Woodpile
No North, No South
Old Daddy Hopkins
Or Any Oder Man's Dog Tacks
Paddy and the Devil War
Parody on "When this Cruel
Patrick's Serenade
Shakspeare Improved
She's Black, but Dat's no Matter
Some Horse
Steamed Oysters, Oh
The Boat Race

The Cure
The Darkey Bachelor
The Darkey's Race
The Dream of the Hard-Up
The End of the World
The Farmer's Boy
The Four Vultures
The Hungry Lover
The Jersey Fisherman
The Lone Fishball
The Men of the Day
The Port Royal Contraband
The Wrong Bill
'Tis the Last Cake of Supper
Up Again and Kiss me Quick
Villkins and His Dinah
Viva l'America
What a Ridiculous Fashion
Why Do I Weep for Thee
Wonderful Transformation
Zouave Johnny's History of Hamlet

CHRISTY'S NEW SONGSTER AND BLACK JOKER.

Acting upon Your Own Conviction
Ain't I Right, eh!
Alabam Again
Annie Lisle
An Expensive Candlestick
Astronomical
A Penny for Your Thoughts
A Sermon
A Ride I Once Was Taking
A Toast
Bad News
Better Times are Coming
Burlesque Stump Oration
Burlesque Political
Canaan
Dat's What's de Matter
De Pretty Yaller Gals
Der Bold Privateer
Ginger Blue

Going a Journey
Horror
I Will Be True to Thee
Jenny's Coming o'er the Green
Kingdom Coming
Money a HardThing to Borrow
"Mother's Love is True"
My Native Town
Our Union None Can Sever
Parsing
Plantation Medley
Poem on Bees
Query
Rock Me to Sleep, Mother
Sally Jones
Shall We Know Each Other There
Stump Speech
Successful
Sweet Love, Forget Me Not

The Crow Family
The Three Crows
The Darkey's Home
The Barber
The Peanut Stand
The Baby Show
The Raw Recruits
The Widow's Victim
Uncle Sam's Cooks
Uncle Sam
Uncle Snow
Vegetable Poetry
Was my Brother in the Battle
Weighing the Question
We'll Gib de White Folks a Concert
Why Have my Loved Ones Gone
Yaller Dine
You Ought to See Us Kitin

Copies mailed to any address in the United States, free of postage, on receipt of Ten Cents.

6

NELSE SEYMOUR'S BIG SHOE SONGSTER.

THE CHARLEY O'MALLEY IRISH SONGSTER.

FRED MAY'S COMIC IRISH SONGSTER.

THE DOUBLE QUICK COMIC SONGSTER.

THE FRISKY IRISH SONGSTER.

An Irishman's Excuse for a
Fight   [Ladies
A Tight Irish Heart for the
Ballinamana Oro
Barrel of Pork
Batch of Cakes
Biddy Maguire of Ballinaclash
Bryan O'Lynn
Cruiskeen Lawn
Dolly Dunn of Donnybrook
Don't You Think She Did
Friend, By my Sowl
Gaffer Gray
Going Home with the Milk
Handy Andy
Hoppy Hoolahan's Lament
Horticultural Wife
Jeff Davis

Larry McHale
Murrough O'Monahan
Murthough Delany's Birth
Nell Flaugherty's Drake
Paddy Goshlow
Paddy's Grave
Pat and the Priest
Petticoat Lane
Robinson Crusoe
Shelah O'Neal
Soldier's Dream
Sprig of Shillelah
Summer Hill Courtship
The Anchor's Weighed
The Bells of Shandon
The Freemason
The Great Big Ugly Irishman
The Guager's Slip

The Humors of Passage
The Hungry Army
The Jolly Beggar
The Land of Shillelah
The Man in the Moon
The Miller's Song
The Muleteer
The New York Volunteer
The Pirate Crew
The Stars and Stripes
The Wedding of Ballyporeen
The Widow that Keeps the
  Cock Inn
The Wild Irishman
There's Room for All
Useful Knowledge   [Leads
What an Illigant Life a Friar
Young Volunteer

GUS SHAW'S COMIC SONGSTER.

Alonzo the Brave
Brogue and Blarney
Shells of Oysters
The Bill Poster
Mr and Mrs Snibbs
Nora Daley
St Patrick's Birthday
The Female Smuggler
The Lively Flea
Sights for a Father
Nepoletaine

My Mother was a True Born
  Irishman
Paper Song
Mr and Mrs Bone
Robin Ruff and Gaffer Green
Root Hog or Dio
Rat Catcher's Daughter
Larboard Watch
Larry O'Brien
The Irishman's Shanty
New York in Slices

Hamlet—A Tragedy
Nonsense
Bumper of Lager
My Mary's Nose
Fair of Clogheen
Billy Nut's the Poet
In the Days When I Was
  Hard Up
The Irish Jaunting Car
Wooden Leg Sailor
The Sicilian Maid

THE TENT AND FORECASTLE SONGSTER.

Abram's Band   [ment
Annie Lisle's Lovyer's La-
A Light at Your Nose
Ben Backstay the Boatswain
Courage, Mother, I'm Going
Dicky Dip the Oilman
Donnybrook Fair
Dat's Wot de "Ledger" Says
Gilhooly the Brave, & McGuf-
Hail to Columbia [fin the Fair
Looncy is Gone
Lord & Taylor's Shopman
Lands for the Landless
Mr Foote, Mr Head and Miss
  Boddy   [of My Coat
Micky Magee; or, the Tail

My Fancy Pants
No Grog in the Navy
New Gideon's Band
On With Our Flag
Old Nick in New York
Our Boarding House
Patrick O'Shannon
Parody on "Ever of Thee'
Pat and the Dutchman
Reefing the Breakers
Scraps of Fun
The Army and Navy
The New Tax Bill
The Female Recruiting Ser-
  geant
The Wonderful Sword

The Irish Volunteers
The Broadway Dandy
The Peanut Stand
The Unfortunate Housekeeper
The Sailor's Pride
The King of Otahelte
The Knock-Kneed Tailor
The Mighty Apple Pudding
The American Tar
The Fancy Peeler
The Beautiful Boy
The Dutchman's Experience
The Union
To My Old Dudheen
When a Lad, With my Dad
Widdy McGinness's Raffle

THE LITTLE MAC SONGSTER.

A Question for Officers
Advertising for a Wife
Anything Green
A Broth of a Boy
Bits of Wit
Billy was a Butcher Boy
Buchanan, He Sate in the
  White House Chair
Columbia, the Hope of the
  World
Columbia Shall Weather the
  Storm
Columbia, the Land of Free-
  dom's Birth
Codfish Balls
De Shoemaker's Boy
Dat's Whar de Hen Scratches
Dates of First Things
For the Flag of His Country
  He Died
Gallant "Little Mac"
Helm and Blade
Il Trovatore
I Wish I Had a Fat Contract

Jeff Davis
Let Her Rip
Long Live McClellan
" Little Mac"
Meagher is Leading the Irish
  Brigade
My Own Native Land
McClellan, the Hope of the
  Nation
Manhood's Diploma
My Father's Gun
New "Marching Along"
New Curiosity Shop
Our Fifer Boy
Our Yankee Generals
Our Own Flag of Green
Oh, Wonderful Man
Playing Billiards
Shakspeare on "Little Mac"
"Stonewall" the Rush
So Forth and So Cu
The Union Volunteers
The Irish Volunteer's Wife
The Confidence Man

The Union Hand of Trumps
The Men of the " Sixty-
  Ninth"
The Days of Washington
The Pretty Girl Selling Hot
  Corn
The Keg of Whisky, O !
The Skeleton Cavalry
The Three Legged Stool
The Excelsior John Brown
The Furloughed Soldier
The Sword of Bunker Hill
The Marseilles Hymn
The Standard Bearer
Tom Brown
Union Boys, Stand to Your
  Guns
Up, Comrades, Up
Undaunted in Peril
We Won't Go Home 'Till
  Morning
When He Comes Back all
  Glorious
Yankee Doodle, " New"

Popular Books sent Free of Postage at the prices annexed.

The Sociable; *or, One Thousand and One Home Amusements.* Containing Acting Proverbs, Dramatic Charades, Acting Charades, Tableaux Vivants, Parlor Games, and Parlor Magic, and a choice collection of Puzzles, &c., illustrated with nearly 300 Engravings and Diagrams, the whole being a fund of never-ending entertainment. By the Author of the "Magician's Own Book." Nearly 400 pages, 12mo., cloth, gilt side stamp................................Price $1.25.

Inquire Within *for Anything You Want to Know; or, Over 3,700 Facts for the People.* Illustrated, 436 large pages...Price $1.25.

"Inquire Within" is one of the most valuable and extraordinary volumes ever presented to the American public, and embodies nearly 4,000 facts, in most of which any person living will find instruction, aid, and entertainment. It contains so many valuable and useful recipes, that an enumeration of them requires *seventy-two columns of fine type for the Index.*

The Corner Cupboard; *or, Facts for Everybody.* By the Author of "Inquire Within," "The Reason Why," &c. Large 12mo., 400 pages, cloth, gilt side and back. Illustrated with over 1000 Engravings.
Price $1.25.

The Reason Why: *General Science.* A careful collection of some thousands of reasons for things, which, though generally known, are imperfectly understood. By the Author of "Inquire Within." A handsome 12mo. volume of 356 pages, cloth, gilt, and embellished with a large number of wood-cuts....................Price $1.25.

The Biblical Reason Why: A Hand-Book for Biblical Students, and a Guide to Family Scripture Readings. By the Author of "Inquire Within, &c. Beautifully illustrated, large 12mo. cloth, gilt side and back..Price $1.25.

The Reason Why: *Natural History.* By the Author of "Inquire Within," "The Biblical Reason Why," &c. 12mo. cloth, gilt side and back. Giving Reasons for hundreds of interesting facts in Natural History...Price $1.25.

10,000 Wonderful Things. Comprising the Marvellous and Rare, Odd, Curious, Quaint, Eccentric, and Extraordinary, in all Ages and Nations, in Art, Nature, and Science. including many Wonders of the world, enriched with Hundreds of Authentic Illustrations. 12mo. cloth, gilt side and back ....Price $1.25.

That's It; *or, Plain Teaching* By the Author of "Inquire Within," "The Reason Why," &c. Illustrated with over 1,200 Wood-cuts. 12mo. cloth, gilt side and back.......................Price $1.25.

The Lady's Manual of Fancy Work A Complete Instructor in every variety of Ornamental Needle-Work; including Shading and Coloring, Printer's Marks, Explanatory Terms, &c., &c. The Whole being a Complete Lexicon of Fancy Work. By Mrs. PULLAN, Director of the Work-table of Frank Leslie's Magazine, &c., &c. Illustrated with over 300 Engravings, by the best Artists, with eight large pattern plates, elegantly printed in colors on tinted paper. Large 8vo., beautifully bound in fine cloth, with gilt side and back stamp.
Price $1.25.

The Secret Out: *or, One Thousand Tricks with Cards and other Recreations.* Illustrated with over Three Hundred Engravings. A book which explains all the Tricks and Deceptions with Playing Cards ever known or invented, and gives, besides, a great many new and interesting ones—the whole being described so accurately and carefully, with engravings to illustrate them, that anybody can easily learn how to practice these Tricks. This work also contains 240 of the best Tricks in Legerdemain, in addition to the card tricks. 12mo, 400 pages, bound in cloth, with gilt side and back..............Price $1 25.

The Art of Dancing. Containing the Figures, Music, and necessary instruction for all Modern Approved Dances. Also, Hints on Etiquette and the Ethics of Politeness. By EDWARD FERRERO, Professor of Dancing, &c. A large bound book, full of Engravings and Music to illustrate it..Price $1.25.

The Dictionary of Love. Containing a Definition of all the terms used in Courtship, with rare quotations from Poets of all Nations, together with specimens of curious Model Love Letters. and many other interesting matters appertaining to Love, never before published. 12mo, cloth, gilt side and back..........................Price $1. 25.

The Magician's Own Book. Being a Hand-Book of Parlor Magic, and containing several hundred amusing Magical, Magnetical, Electrical, and Chemical Experiments, Astonishing Transmutations, Wonderful Sleight-of-Hand and Card Tricks, Curious and Perplexing Puzzles, Quaint Questions in Numbers, &c., together with all the most noted Tricks of Modern Performers. Illustrated with over 500 Wood Engravings. 12mo, cloth, gilt side and back stamp, 400 pages.
Price $1. 25.

The Book of 1,000 Tales and Amusing Adventures. Containing over 300 Engravings, and 450 pages. This is a magnificent book, and is crammed full of narratives and adventures........Price $1.00.

The Bordeaux Wine and Liquor Dealer's Guide; *or, How to Manufacture and Adulterate Liquors.* By a practical Liquor Manufacturer. 12mo, cloth....................................Price $2 00.

In this work, *not one* article in the smallest degree approximating to a poison is recommended, and yet the book teaches how Cognac Brandy, Scotch and Irish Whiskey, Foreign and Domestic Rum, all kinds of Wines, Cordials, &c., from the choicest to the commonest, can be imitated to that perfection that the best judges cannot detect the method of manufacture, even by chemical tests of the severest character.

Ladies' Guide to Crochet. By Mrs. ANN S. STEPHENS. Copiously illustrated with original and very choice designs in Crochet, etc., printed in colors, separate from the letter press, on tinted paper. Also with numerous wood-cuts, printed with the letter press, explanatory of terms, etc. Oblong, pp 117, beautifully bound in extra cloth, gilt, This is by far the best work on the subject of Crochet ever published.
Price $1 00

Arts of Beauty ; *or, Secrets of a Lady's Toilet.* With Hints to Gentlemen on the Art of Fascinating. By Madame LOLA MONTEZ, Countess of Landsfeldt. Cloth, gilt side. This book contains an account, in detail, of all the arts employed by the fashionable ladies of all the chief cities of Europe, for the purpose of developing and preserving their charms .... Price 50 cts.

Popular Books sent Free of Postage at the prices annexed.

Live and Learn: A Guide for all those who wish to speak and write correctly; particularly intended as a Book of Reference for the solution of difficulties connected with Grammar, Composition, Punctuation, &c., &c., containing examples of one thousand mistakes of daily occurrence, in speaking, writing, and pronunciation. 216 pages, cloth, 12mo..Price 63 cts.

The Harp of a Thousand Strings; or, *Laughter for a Lifetime.* A large book of nearly 400 pages. By the Author of Mrs. Partington's Carpet-Bag of Fun." Bound in a handsome gilt cover. Containing more than a million laughs, and crowded full of Funny Stories, besides being illustrated with over Two Hundred Comical Engravings, by Darley, McLennan, Bellew, &c.....................Price $1.25.

The Book of 1,000 Comical Stories; or, *Endless Repast of Fun,* Appropriately illustrated with 300 Comic Engravings. By the Author of "Mrs. Partington's Carpet Bag of Fun." Large 12mo. cloth.
Price $1.00.

The Perfect Gentleman: or, *Etiquette and Eloquence.* A Book of Information and Instruction for those who desire to become brilliant and conspicuous in General Society; or at Parties, Dinners, or Popular Gatherings. Containing Model Speeches for all Occasions, with Directions how to deliver them; 500 Toasts and Sentiments for everybody, and their proper mode of introduction; How to use Wine at Table; with Rules for judging the quality of Wine, and Rules for Carving; Etiquette, or proper Behavior in Company, with an American Code of Politeness for every Occasion; Etiquette at Washington, Remarkable Wit and Conversation at Table, &c., &c. To which is added, The Duties of a Chairman of a Public Meeting, with Rules for the Orderly Conduct thereof; together with Valuable Hints and Examples for Drawing up Preambles and Resolutions, and a great deal of instructive and amusing matter never before published. 12mo. cloth, nearly 400 pages...Price $1.25.

Songs of Ireland: Embracing Songs of the Affections, Convivial and Comic Songs, Patriotic and Military Songs; Historical and Political Songs; Moral, Sentimental, Satirical, and Miscellaneous Songs. Edited and Annotated by SAMUEL LOVER, Author of "Handy Andy," "Rory O More," "Legends and Stories of Ireland," &c. Embellished with numerous fine Illustrations, engraved by the celebrated Dalziel. 12mo. cloth, gilt side and back...........................Price $1.25.

Narratives and Adventures of Travelers in Africa. By Charles Williams, Esq. 12mo. cloth, gilt back. Profusely illustrated with Engravings..Price $1.00.

The Lady's Own Pattern Book; or, *Treasures in Needlework.* Comprising instructions in Knitting, Netting, Crochet, Point Lace, Tatting, Braiding, Embroidery, &c. Illustrated with over Five Hundred Useful and Ornamental Designs, Patterns, &c. By Mrs. PULLAN and Mrs. WARREN. Large 12mo. gilt side and back. This work, which is superbly gotten up, so as to fit it for holiday *souvenirs*, contains over Five Hundred Engravings, Pattern Plates, &c., and besides, embraces minute instructions for the execution of every known species of needle-work. No family should be without it.........Price $1.25.

Anecdotes of Love. Being a true account of the most remarkable events connected with the History of Love in all Ages and among all Nations. By LOLA MONTEZ, Countess of Landsfeldt. Large 12mo, cloth.
Price $1.25.

Send cash orders to **Dick & Fitzgerald, 18 Ann St., N. Y.**

Popular Books sent Free of Postage at the prices annexed.

Every Woman Her Own Lawyer. A private Guide in all matters of Law, of essential interest to Women, and by the aid of which every Female may, in whatever situation, understand her legal course and redress, and be her own Legal Adviser. By GEORGE BISHOP. Large 12mo, nearly 400 pages, bound in half leather. This book should be in the hands of every woman, young or old, married or single, in the United States..Price $1 00.

Richardson's Monitor of Free-Masonry: A Complete Guide to the various Ceremonies and Routine in Free-Masons' Lodges, Chapters, Encampments, Hierarchies, &c., &c., in all the Degrees, whether Modern, Ancient, Ineffable, Philosophical, or Historical. Containing, also, the Signs, Tokens, Grips, Pass-words, Decorations, Drapery. Dress, Regalia, and Jewels, in each Degree. Profusely illustrated with Explanatory Engravings, Plans of the Interior of Lodges, &c, By JABEZ RICHARDSON, A. M. A book of 185 pages.
Bound in paper covers ....Price 50 cts.
Bound and gilt ....Price 75 cts.
This is the only book ever written which gives a detailed description of all the doings inside a Masonic meeting.

The Manufacture of Liquors, Wines, and Cordials. Without the aid of Distillation; also, the Manufacture of Effervescing Beverages, and Syrups, Vinegar, and Bitters. Prepared and arranged expressly for the Trade. Py PIERRE LACOUR. Procure a copy of "Lacour on the Manufacture of Liquors," or if you do not wish to purchase, look through the book for a few moments as a matter of curiosity. Physicians' and Druggists' pharmaceutical knowledge cannot be complete without a copy of this work. 12mo, cloth...........Price $2 00.

Mrs. Partington's Carpet-Bag of Fun. A Collection of over one thousand of the most comical stories, amusing adventures, side-splitting jokes, cheek-extending poetry, funny conundrums. QUEER SAYINGS OF MRS. PARTINGTON, heart-rending puns, witty repartees, etc., etc. The whole illustrated by about 150 comic wood cuts.
12mo, 300 pages, cloth, gilt.....................Price $1 00
Ornamented paper covers......................Price 50 cts.

Sam Slick in Search of a Wife. 12mo, paper.........Price 50 cts.
Cloth ....Price $1 00
Everybody has heard of "Sam Slick, the Clockmaker," and he has given his opinion on almost everything.

Sam Slick's Nature and Human Nature. Large 12mo.
Paper ....Price 50 cts.
Cloth.....................................Price $1 00

The Attachee: or, Sam Slick in England. Large 12mo.
Paper ....Price 50 cts.
Cloth.....................................Price $1 00

Sam Slick's Sayings and Doings. Paper...........Price 50 cts.
Cloth.....................................Price $1 C0

The Game of Draughts, or Checkers, Simplified and Explained. With Practical Diagrams and Illustrations, together with a Checker board, numbered and printed in red. Containing the Eighteen Standard Games, with over 200 of the best variations, selected from the various authors, together with many original ones never before published. By D. SCATTERGOOD. Bound in cloth, with flexible cover.....................................Price 38 cts.

Send cash orders to **Dick & Fitzgerald, 18 Ann St., N. Y.**

The Book of 500 Curious Puzzles. Containing a large collection of Entertaining Paradoxes, Perplexing Deceptions in Numbers and Amusing Tricks in Geometry. By the author of "The Sociable." Illustrated with a great variety of engravings. 12mo, fancy paper cover......................................Price 25 cts.

The Book of Fireside Games: A Repertory of Social Amusements. Containing an Explanation of the most Entertaining Games, suited to the Family Circle as a Recreation. By the Author of "The Sociable," "The Secret Out," &c., &c. Illustrated, 12mo, fancy paper cover......................................Price 25 cts.

The American Home Cook-Book. Containing several hundred excellent Recipes. The whole based on many years' experience of an American Housewife. Illustrated with Engravings. All the Recipes in this Book are written from actual experiments in Cooking. There are no copyings from theoretical cooking recipes. It is a book of 128 pages, and is very cheap......................Price 25 cts.

Dr. Valentine's Comic Lectures. A budget of Wit and Humor; or, Morsels of Mirth for the Melancholy. A certain cure for the blues, and all other serious complaints. Comprising Comic Lectures on Heads, Faces, Noses, Mouths, Animal Magnetism, etc., with Specimens of Eloquence, Transactions of Learned Societies, Delineations of Eccentric Characters, Comic Songs, etc,, etc. By Dr. W. VALENTINE, the favorite delineator of Eccentric Characters. Illustrated with twelve portraits of Dr. Valentine, in his most celebrated characters. 12mo, cloth, gilt...........................Price 75 cts.
Ornamental paper cover.....................Price 50 cts.

Dr. Valentine's Comic Metamorphoses. Being the second series of Dr. Valentine's Lectures, with characters as given by the late Yankee Hill. Embellished with numerous portraits. Ornamental paper cover............................Price 50 cts.
Cloth, gilt......................................Price 75 cts.

The Book of 1,000 Comical Stories; or, *Endless Repast of Fun.* A rich banquet for every day in the year, with several courses and a dessert. BILL OF FARE: Comprising Tales of Humor, Laughable Anecdotes, Irresistible Drol'eries, Jovial Jokes, Comical Conceits, Puns and Pickings, Quibbles and Queries, Bon Mots and Broadgrins, Oddities, Epigrams, &c., &c. Appropriately Illustrated with 300 Comic Engravings. By the author of "Mrs. Partington's Carpet-Bag of Fun." Large 12mo, cloth..........................Price $1.00.

The Courtship and Adventures of Jonathan Homebred; *or, the Scrapes and Escapes of a Live Yankee.* Beautifully Illustrated. 12mo, cloth. The book is printed in handsome style, on good paper, and with amusing engravings....................Price $1.00.

Etiquette and the Usages of Society. Containing the most Approved Rules for Correct Conduct in Social and Fashionable Life—with Hints to both Gentlemen and Ladies on Awkward and Vulgar Habits. Also, the Etiquette of Love and Courtship, Marriage Etiquette, &c., &c. By H. P. WILLIS. A book of 64 pages........Price 10 cts. Bound in cloth with gilt side, and printed on fine paper, suitable for a present to a lady........................Price 25 cts.

The Chairman and Speaker's Guide; or, *Rules for the Orderly Conduct of Public Meetings.*..........................Price 12 cts.

Pettengill's Perfect Fortune-Teller and Dream-Book: *or, The Art of Discerning Future Events,* as practiced by Modern Seers and Astrologers—being also a Key to the Hidden Mysteries of the Middle Ages. To which is added Curious and Amusing Charms, Invocations, Signs, &c., &c. By PELETIAH PETTENGILL, Philom. A book of 144 pages, bound in boards, with cloth back .... Price 30 cts.

Courtship Made Easy; *or, The Art of Making Love fully Explained.* Containing full and minute directions for conducting a Courtship with Ladies of every age and position in society, and valuable information for persons who desire to enter the marriage state. Also, Forms of Love Letters to be used on certain occasions. 64 pp. **Price 12 cts.**

Chesterfield's Art of Letter-writing Simplified. A Guide to Friendly, Affectionate, Polite, and Business Correspondence....Price 12 cts.

Containing a large collection of the most valuable information relative to the Art of Letter-Writing, with clear and complete instructions how to begin and end correspondence, Rules for Punctuation and Spelling, &c., together with numerous examples of Letters and Notes on every subject of Epistolary Intercourse, with several Important Hints on Love Letters.

Knowlson's Farrier, *and Complete Horse Doctor.* We have printed a new and revised edition of this celebrated book, which contains Knowlsons famous Recipe for the cure of Spavin, and other new matter. It is positively the best book of the kind ever written. We sell it cheap because of the immense demand for it. The farmers and horsekeepers like it because it gives them plain common-sense directions how to manage their horses. We sell our new edition (64 pages, 18mo,) cheap .... Price 12 cts.

The Art of Conversation: With Remarks on Fashion and Address. By MRS. MABERLY. This is the best book on the subject ever published. It contains nothing that is verbose or difficult to understand, but all the instructions and rules for conversation are given in a plain and common-sense manner, so that any one, however dull, can easily comprehend them. 64 pages octavo, large........... Price 25 cts.

Horse-Taming by a New Method, *as Practiced by J. S. Rarey.* A New and Improved Edition, containing Mr. Rarey's whole Secret of Subduing and Breaking Vicious Horses, together with his Improved Plan of Managing Young Colts, and Breaking them to the Saddle, the Harness, and the Sulkey—with ten engravings illustrating the process. Every person who keeps a horse should buy this book. It costs but a trifle, and you will positively find it an excellent guide in the management of that noble animal. This is a very handsome book of 64 pages .... Price 12 cts.

The Game of Whist: Rules, Directions and Maxims to be observed in playing it. Containing also Primary Rules for Beginners, Explanations and Directions for Old Players, and the Laws of the Game. Compiled from Hoyle and Matthews. Also, Loo, Euchre, and Poker, as now generally played—with an explanation of Marked Cards, &c., &c.. Price 12 cts.

The Young Bride's Book: An Epitome of the Social and Domestic Duties of Woman, as the Wife and the Mother. By ARTHUR FREEING. This is one of the best and most useful books ever issued in the cheap form. It is printed in clear and beautiful type, and on fine paper.. Price 12 cts.

The Ladies' Love Oracle ; *or, Counsellor to the Fair Sex.* Being a complete Fortune Teller and Interpreter to all questions upon the different events and situations of life, but more especially relating to all circumstances connected with Love, Courtship, and Marriage. By MADAME LE MARCHAND. Beautifully illustrated cover, printed in colors..Price 25 cts.

The Laws of Love. A complete Code of Gallantry.
12 mo. Paper ....Price 25 cts.
Containing concise rules for the conduct of Courtship through its entire progress, aphorisms of love, rules for telling the characters and dispositions of women, remedies for love, and an Epistolary Code.

Gamblers' Tricks with Cards Exposed and Explained. By J. H. GREEN, Reformed Gambler. 12mo, paper..........Price 25 cts.
This work contains one hundred tricks with cards, explained, and shows the numerous cheats which Gamblers practice upon their unwary dupes.

How to Win and How to Woo. Containing Rules for the Etiquette of Courtship, with directions showing how to win the favor of Ladies, how to begin and end a Courtship, and how Love Letters should be written.......................................Price 12 cts.

Bridal Etiquette. A Sensible Guide to the Etiquette and Observances of the Marriage Ceremonies; containing complete directions for Bridal Receptions, and the necessary rules for bridesmaids, groomsmen sending cards, &c., &c..........................Price 12 cts.

How to Behave ; *or, The Spirit of Etiquette.* A Complete Guide to Polite Society, for Ladies and Gentlemen ; containing rules for good behavior at the dinner table, in the parlor, and in the street ; with important hints on introduction, conversation, &c....Price 12 cts.

The Everlasting Fortune-Teller and Magnetic Dream-Book. Containing the science of foretelling events by the Signs of the Zodiac, Lists of Lucky and Unlucky Days, with Presages drawn therefrom ; the science of Foretelling Events by cards, dice, &c...Price 25 cts.

Morgan's Free-Masonry Exposed and Explained. Showing the Origin, History, and Nature of Masonry; its Effects on the Government and the Christian Religion; and containing a Key to all the Degrees of Free-Masonry ; giving a clear and correct view of the manner of Conferring the Different Degrees, as practiced in all Lodges throughout the Globe ....Price 25 cts.

How to Dress with Taste ; Containing hints on the harmony of colors, the theory of contrast, the complexion, shape or hight, Price 12 cts.

Mind Your Stops: Punctuation made plain, and Composition simplified for Readers, Writers and Talkers..............Price 12 cts.
This little book is worth ten times the price asked for it, and will teach accurately in everything, from the diction of a friendly letter to the composition of a learned treatise.

Hard Words Made Easy ; Rules for Pronunciation and Accent ; with instructions how to pronounce French, Italian, German, Russian, Danish, Dutch, Swedish, Norwegian, and other foreign names. A capital work ....Price 12 cts.

Courteney's Dictionary of Abbreviations: Literary, Scientific, Commercial, Ecclesiastical, Military, Naval, Legal and Medical. A book of reference—3,000 abbreviations—for the solution of all literary mysteries. By EDWARD S. C. COURTENEY, Esq. This is a very useful book. Everybody should get a copy...........Price 12 cts.

Blunders in Behavior Corrected......................Price 12 cts.
A concise code of deportment for both sexes. "It will polish and refine either sex, and is Chesterfield superseded.—*Home Companion.*

Five Hundred French Phrases. Adapted for those who aspire to speak and write French correctly.............................Price 12 cts.

How to detect Adulteration in our Daily Food and Drink. A complete analysis of the frauds and deceptions practiced upon articles of consumption, by storekeepers and manufacturers; with full directions to detect genuine from spurious, by simple and inexpensive means..Price 12 cts.

The Young Housekeeper's Book; *or, How to have a Good Living upon a Small Income*.................................Price 12 cts.

How to be Healthy: Being a complete Guide to Long Life. By a Retired Physician.....................................Price 12 cts.

How to Cut and Contrive Children's Clothes at a Small Cost With numerous explanatory engravings....................Price 12 cts.

How to Talk and Debate; *or, Fluency of Speech Attained without the Sacrifice of Elegance and Sense,*....................Price 12 cts.

How to Manage Children.............................Price 12 cts.

The Great Wizard of the North's Hand-Book of Natural Magic. Being a series of the newest Tricks of Deception, arranged for Amateurs and Lovers of the Art. By Professor J. H. ANDERSON, the Great Wizard of the North............................Price 25 cts.

The Knapsack full of Fun; *or,* 1000 *Rations of Laughter.* Illustrated with over 500 Comical Engravings, and containing over 1000 Jokes and Funny Stories by "DOESTICKS," and other witty writers. Large Quarto...Price 25 cts.

The Plate of Chowder; *A Dish for Funny Fellows.* Appropriately illustrated with 100 Comic Engravings. By the Author of "Mrs. Partington's Carpet-Bag of Fun." 12mo, paper cover....Price 25 cts.

Deacon Doolittle's Drolleries. A Collection of Funny and Laughable Stories told by the Deacon, in which he had either acted a part or taken much interest in. This book is got up especially for the benefit of thin and spare people—or for that class of mankind whom it would benefit to "Laugh and Grow Fat." It contains some thirty or forty of the best stories ever invented, full of droll and laughable incidents, calculated to drive away the blues, and to make one in good humor with all mankind..Price 12 cts.

The Laughable Adventures of Messrs. Brown, Jones, & Robinson, showing where they went, and how they went; what they did, and how they did it. With nearly two hundred most thrillingly-comic engravings......................................Price 25 cts.

Fontaine's Golden Wheel Dream-Book and Fortune-Teller. By FELIX FONTAINE, Fortune-Teller and Astrologer. Being the most complete book on Fortune-Telling and Interpreting Dreams ever printed. Each Dream has the LUCKY NUMBER which the Dream signifies attached to it, and those who wish to purchase Lottery Tickets will do well to consult them. This book also informs you how to TELL FORTUNES with the *Golden Wheel*, with *Cards, Dice,* and *Dominoes;* how to tell future events by Psalmistry on the lines of the hands, by moles on the body, by the face, nails, and shape of the head; how to find where to dig for water, coal, and all kinds of metals, with the celebrated DIVINING ROD; Charms to make your Sweetheart love you, to make your Lover pop the question; together with Twenty Ways of Telling Fortunes on New Year's Eve. This book contains 144 pages, and is bound in pasteboard sides with cloth back. It is illustrated with numerous Engravings, showing how to hold the Divining Rod, how to lay out Cards when you Tell Fortunes, how to tell the names of your intended Wife or Husband by the charm of the Key and Book, etc. This book also contains a large Colored Lithographic Engraving of the *Golden Wheel,* which folds up. It is the cheapest on our list------------------**Price 30 cts.**

Chesterfield's Letter-Writer and Complete Book of Etiquette; or, *Concise Systematic Directions for Arranging and Writing Letters.* Also, Model Correspondence in Friendship and Business, and a great variety of Model' ove Letters. If any lady or gentleman desires to know how to begin a Love Correspondence, this is just the book they want. If they wish to speak their minds to a tardy, a bashful, or a careless or indifferent lover, or sweetheart, this book tells exactly how it should be done. This work is also a Complete Book of Etiquette. You will find more real information in this book than in half-a-dozen volumes of the more expensive ones. It is emphatically a book for the million, and one which every young person should have. As it contains Etiquette for Ladies, as well as for Gentlemen—Etiquette of Courtship and Marriage—Etiquette for writing Love Letters, and all that sort of thing, it is an appropriate book to present to a lady. This book contains 136 pages, and is bound in pasteboard sides, with cloth back------------------**Price 30 cts.**

Le Marchand's Fortune-Teller and Dream-Book. A complete interpretation to all questions upon the different events and situations of life; but more especially relating to *Love, Courtship and Marriage.* .Containing the significations of all the various Dreams, together with numerous other methods of foretelling future events. By MADAM LE MARCHAND, the celebrated Parisian Fortune-Teller---------------------------------------**Price 30 cts.**

100 Tricks With Cards. J. H. Green, the Reformed Gambler, has just authorized the publication of a new edition of his book entitled, "Gamblers' Tricks with Cards Exposed and Explained." This is a book of 95 pages, and it exposes and explains all the mysteries of the Gambling Tables. It is interesting not only to those who play, but to those who do not. Old Players will get some new ideas from this curious book--**Price 25 cts.**

Laughing Gas. An Encyclopædia of Wit, Wisdom, and Wind. By SAM SLICK, Jr. Comically illustrated with 100 original and laughable Engravings, and nearly 500 side-extending Jokes, and other things to get fat on; and the best of it is, that every thing about the book is new and fresh—all new—new designs, new stories, new type —no comic almanac stuff. It will be found a complete antidote to "hard times"--**Price 25 cts.**

www.ingramcontent.com/pod-product-compliance
Lightning Source LLC
Chambersburg PA
CBHW031445270326
41930CB00007B/876